D0260200

ANE SATYRE OF THE THRIE ESTAITS

ANE SATYRE OF THE THRIE ESTAITES

Sir David Lyndsay of the Mount

Acting text by ROBERT KEMP

AN EDINBURGH INTERNATIONAL FESTIVAL PRODUCTION
with the collaboration of
SCOTTISH THEATRE COMPANY

Polygon Books

Revised edition first published in Great Britain 1985 by Polygon Books, Edinburgh EH8 9LW.

The copyright owner of the Acting Text by Robert Kemp is the Literary Executor, Mr Derek Glynne, care of The London Company (International Plays) Ltd., 25 Haymarket, London SW1Y 4EN, England, to whom enquiries regarding all performing rights should be made.

Typeset by E.U.S.P.B.
Printed by Martins of Berwick

ISBN 0 948275 06 5

The Publisher acknowledges subsidy from the Scottish Arts Council towards the publication of this volume.

FOREWORD

Sir David Lyndsay, son of David Lyndsay of the Mount, a small estate in Fife, was born in 1486. By the time he was 25, he was serving at the court of King James the Fourth, perhaps Scotland's most charismatic monarch. It was a brilliant and cosmopolitan court. The king was a lover of the arts, interested in science and medicine, and spoke six languages fluently. Young David Lyndsay took part in the masques and interludes performed for his king's diversion. When James, and most of the flower of Scotland's nobility, were killed in Flodden field in 1513, Lyndsay became gentleman-usher to the infant James V. For ten years he was friend and servant to the boy-king, falling out of favour with the rise to power of the Earl of Angus. The young king escapéd from the clutches of his step-father in 1528, and Lyndsay increasingly became an influential personage at court. By 1530 he was a herald, entrusted with diplomatic missions to the courts of Europe. By 1542 he had been knighted on his appointment as Lyon King of Arms, the supreme heraldic officer in Scotland whose work incorporates that of the Earl Marshal and Lord Chamberlain in England, viz. the organizing of all State ceremonial.

Lyndsay was also a poet. Some have reckoned him to be "the one Scots poet before Burns to reach all classes". Certainly, although he was a courtier and, as such, involved at the centre of Scottish 'establishment' affairs, he never lost touch with 'the people' or the ordinary man's struggle for justice and fair treatment. His poems are filled with love of Scotland and a concern for its welfare. He pleads with the King he knew as a child not to abuse his high office. He ridicules the excesses of the Church. (His home county of Fife was the centre of a campaign for ecclesiastical reform). In his greatest work *Ane Satyre of the Thrie Estaites* he mercilessly attacks the morals of the Court, the abuses within the Church, and the evils of Society at large, and he does so with immense energy and wit. Is there another nation in 16th Century Europe where a playright could have been so outspoken (before an audience which included the Sovereign and his consort, the nobility, and the hierarchy of the Church) and got away with his life? Will Shakespeare, writing for James V's grandson sixty years on, was much more circumspect in moulding history for the flattery and pleasure of his royal Patron.

Lyndsay's *Satyre*, in the form of a simple morality, was first performed on Twelfth Night, 1540, within Linlithgow Palace. It was performed two years later in an extended version on the Castle Hill at Cupar (three miles from Lyndsay's home), and more than a decade later it was performed at the Playfield on Calton Hill in Edinburgh on 12th August 1554 (in a version which, with intervals, is said to have lasted nine hours!). Sir David Lyndsay died a year later, and, three years after his demise, at the behest of an outraged clergy the play was ordered to be burned by the public executioner.

As far as we know, the 1554 performance was the last to be seen in Edinburgh until the celebrated production by Tyrone Guthrie of Robert Kemp's cleverly abridged acting text in the Assembly Hall of the Church of Scotland during the Second Edinburgh International Festival in 1948. Guthrie's re-invention of a three-level Elizabethan thrust stage, its shape somewhat determined by the permanent furniture of the Hall, laid the foundation for a 20th Century revolution in theatre presentation which has become world-wide in the past fifty years. On Guthrie's long, narrow Assembly Hall stage, thrusting into the auditorium and surrounded on three sides by audience, the actor standing on one side of the stage is never more than twelve feet from the audience on the other side. The great joy of Guthrie's revolution for the actor — still more so for the director — is that all the old ground-rules suddenly become irrelevant. 'Upstage' and 'downstage' and 'scissor crosses' and 'masking' — the Highway Code of proscenium-arch acting (and all the dreadful production clichés that go with it) have to be abandoned. There are exciting possibilities of liberation for actors' bodies and actors' brains. Guthrie's revolution at the Assembly Hall spilled over to the audience, who found they were part of the proceedings, the confidants of clown and commoner, Vice and Virtue, as the high-spirited action and solemn pageantry swept up the aisles in their midst. How David Lyndsay, bit-player and director of ceremonial would have loved it!

The Guthrie magic was to be seen quickening the Kemp text to life at subsequent Edinburgh Festivals in 1949, 1951 and 1959. In 1973, Bill Bryden used another adaptation including scenes and characters omitted from the previous productions. To my mind, although an interesting exercise, this only emphasized the wisdom and subtlety of Robert Kemp's judicious pruning. For the 1984 production I decided to return to this proven text, using Cedric Thorpe Davie's music which had been a linking feature of all five previous productions. I made some minor alterations and some re-instatements. The ending of the Lord Chamberlain's role as watchdog of public morals, in the twenty-five years since the text had last been used, enabled me to put back a few bawdy speeches cut from the original. I added a song for Sensualitie in Part II, based loosely on some words by Robert Henryson. John Grundy set it to music splendidly.

The world has changed considerably since 1948. When honesty and morality were qualities generally accepted as praiseworthy, it was quite funny and daring to caricature Dames Veritie and Chastitie as a bullying lady missionary and a starchy Hospital matron. Now that honesty and chastity seem little more than quaint and amusing bygones, it is important to take the fragility but indestructability of truth, and the desirability of self-discipline a little more seriously. Now that our lives are controlled by computers, multi-nationals, and the

IMF it also seems right that the two Temporal Estaites (the lords and the merchants) become faceless men hidden under masks. The impoverishment of the spirit in the Third Estait (Spiritualitie or The Church) shows in the glittering richness of the outward trappings and the giddy heights of the towering mitres. Young Humanitie similarly makes up for a lack of Kingly qualities with a robe that is so long and cumbersome that he has difficulty in changing direction. When the Clowns/Vices dress up as clerics they are at once accepted as "men of good". When the Bishop, the Abbot, and the Parson are stripped of their finery they become ridiculous and common-place and are laughed off the stage. Divine Correction, who arrives at the end of Part One (just in time to save Humanitie's realm from ruin) comes surrounded by flags. In previous productions they bore human heraldic devices. In 1984 they are made of elemental colours of Sun, Sea, and Sky. When, at Correction's command, John the Common-Weal (spokesman for common man) is received into the King's Parliament, he is given a robe which resembles a patchwork of all the rich garments taken from the overbearing prelates. The ex-President of the N.U.M. goes uneasily to the House of Lords!

Nadine Baylis, my designer, has worked a miracle with her setting of the play. We have kept the Guthrie thrust stage exactly as it has always been except for the gilding of its upper reaches and the crumbling decay of the lower steps which the Fourth Estait — the Poor People — inhabit. She has, however, used the Hall in a totally innovative way. The gallery for Spiritualitie is laid on top of what is the Royal Gallery during the General Assembly of the Church of Scotland. The other two Estaites sit in the adjacent galleries on either side. There are no coyly curtained alcoves for the dalliance of the courtiers. The acting stage is thus clear of tiresome obstructions, giving the audience its most unimpeded view of the action ever. Falsehood and Deceit are hanged from gibbets made from the roof-beams of the Gallery. Guthrie's court-room tables in Part Two have been eliminated. A simple throne, two stools, and a scattering of cushions is the extent of the furnishings. Diligence, the Master of Ceremonies, sits not in a stall on the stage itself. He is amongst the front row of the audience.

The run of this production opened on the evening of 12th August 1984, 430 years to the day after the *Satyre's* first Edinburgh performance. By permission of the present Lord Lyon King of Arms, the banner of Sir David Lyndsay of the Mount flew from the tower outside, high above The Mound. If this acting text by Robert Kemp remains always for me peopled by the familiar shades of erstwhile colleagues from the Scottish Theatre, it belongs now equally to a new generation of friends in the Scottish Theatre Company, whose bright talents brought it so vividly to life again, before my eyes, in the golden summer days of 1984.

TOM FLEMING.

ROBERT KEMP

Robert Kemp, the Scottish playwright and novelist, was born on the Orkney Island of Hoy, on 25 February 1908, but his family were not Orcadians. For many generations the Kemps were weavers, settled first at the village of Spott, southeast of Edinburgh, and later in the city itself. By the middle of the nineteenth century they were making a modest contribution to Scottish intellectual life; his grandfather, William Strathhenry Kemp, was successively rector of Falkirk Grammar School and head classical master of Glasgow High School.

Robert Kemp remained in Orkney, where his father was Church of Scotland minister at Langhope, until the outbreak of the First World War, when the family moved to Millbrex, and then Birse, near Aboyne, in Aberdeenshire. He went to Aberdeen University and then joined the Manchester Guardian in 1929, the last member of staff to be appointed by its famous editor, C. P. Scott. In 1937, he joined the BBC, working in the Features and Drama Department. *The Country Mouse Goes To Town*, a dramatisation of Henryson's fable, was an instant success when it was broadcast in 1938.

It had always been his ambition to return to his roots in Edinburgh, a city he admired and loved. In 1942 he settled there permanently, remaining with the BBC until 1948, and became one of the outstanding talents associated with the post-war Scottish literary renaissance. He was responsible for many innovative BBC productions, and at the same time had begun to write for the theatre. *Whuppity Stoorie*, performed at Gladstone's Land in Edinburgh in 1944, was followed by *Seven Bottles For The Maestro* (1945) and *A Tramp For Jericho* (1947). *The Saxon Saing*, about Queen Margaret (1949) and *The King Of Scots* (1951), about Robert the Bruce, were performed in the Nave of Dunfermline Abbey.

He was a central figure at early Edinburgh International Festivals, and his adaptation of Sir David Lyndsay's *The Three Estaites* (directed by Tyrone Guthrie, with music by Cedric Thorpe Davie) was the sensation of the second Festival in 1948. He discovered the Church of Scotland General Assembly Hall as a location for threatre-in-the-round, a discovery that had a profound impact on theatre world-wide. And he coined the phrase "Festival Fringe" to describe the multifarious theatre groups that began performing alongside the official Festival. His adaptation of *The Three Estaits* was revived at three subsequent Festivals, and other Assembly Hall successes included *The Highland Fair* and *Hail Caledonia*.

His ambition, however, was to found a permanent Scottish theatre in Edinburgh, and this was realised in 1953 with the founding of the Edinburgh Gateway Company, of which he was the first chairman. The company was the dominant force in Scottish theatre between 1953 and 1965, when it became the Edinburgh Civic Theatre. The creation of a modern Scottish theatre that could handle contemporary themes with confidence was a daunting task. His plays with historical settings like *The Scientific Singers* (1949) and *The Other Dear Chamber* (1951) remained immensely popular and were frequently performed, as were his Moliere translations *Let Wives Tak Tent* (L'Ecole des Femmes) (1948) and *The Laird O' Grippy* (L'Avare) (1958). But *The Asset*, a one-act play of violence and exploitation in a modern working-class setting was ferciously attacked by the Ayr presbytery of the Church of Scotland when it was screened on television in 1952. (Perhaps predictably, many members of the presbytery had not seen the play they were attacking). Almost certainly because of his Church of Scotland background, Kemp reacted strongly to the criticism. He left the Church of Scotland (rejoining after a year) and the incident left a permanent scar. It was, perhaps, in an effort to make amends that the Church invited him to write the official play for the quatercenenary of the Scottish Reformation, *Master John Knox*, in 1960.

In addition to his theatrical output, which amounted to more than 30 plays by the time of his death in 1967, he continued to write for radio and television. He was also a prolific journalist, contributing television criticism and numerous Editorial Diaries, many of them strongly autobiographical, to "The Glasgow Herald". He also wrote five novels. His importance in Scottish theatrical history lies in the crucial part he played in reviving popular interest in a Scottish theatre played in the Scottish language.

His successful radio series *The Guid Scots Tongue* and *The Place Names Of Scotland* another facet of his commitment to Scots as a viable independent language. Above all, the Scots he used, and for which he proselytised, was neither synthetic nor plastic. It was a living language — the language he spoke as a child in Orkney and Aberdeenshire.

NOTES ON THE SPEECH
(for the 1959 production)

This version is derived from the two extant as printed in the Scottish Text Society's edition — the Bannatyne MS and the Charteris Quarto. Its aim is not scholarliness, though I have tried not to do violence to Lyndsay, but to provide an actable text for the special conditions, in language sayable by the actors and easily understood by an audience, even one including many visitors to Scotland.

In point of fact most of Lyndsay's difficulties are purely of the eye — they depend on strange spellings — and once he is written out again in a more modern style they vanish automatically. One or two difficulties remain and these call for discretion on the part of the actor. For example, the ending — *ion* was written *-ioun* and pronounced as two syllables. To keep rhythm the actor must lightly touch in a second syllable, thus effecting an acceptable compromise between the old and the new pronunciations. In many two syllabled words of French origin, like "pleasure" and "courage", he will find that in Lyndsay's day the stress was on the second syllable and again a compromise must be effected. Occasionally syllables now mute have to be given some value — the old Scots plural *-is* for example, which I have written — *ës* to indicate that it is a very light "*e*". Sometimes as in "commandement" a diaeresis shows that the syllable must be touched in. It will generally be obvious from rhymes that some words written as in modern English "die" and "lie" must be pronounced as in Scots "dee" and "lee" (in this I follow a recent standardised fashion of writing Scots). The present participle in Scots ends *-and,* and the verbal noun in *-ing*. I have followed the spelling *-and* or *an'* (the "d" can clearly be elided except where it makes a rhyme) because the difference is a real one, the *-an'* of modern Scots speech being quite different from the *-in'* of the English "huntin'", "shootin'" variety. I suggest that *-and* is sometimes useful in royal and ceremonious speeches, but that in more ordinary tirades it should become *an'*. "Ane" for "one" is again useful for ceremonial or emphasis. It may mean "one" is again useful for ceremonial or emphasis. It may mean "one" or "An" or simply "a". In this version I have cut it a good deal but I have left it where it might have some use.

Lyndsay was a careless metrist, or so editors say, but he also had in his blood the old accented alliterative verse which was displaced by rhyme. Often when a line seems bad by conventional ideas of metre, it sounds well if one follows the stresses, which may fall a little irregularly.

Robert Kemp.

This is a working text derived from several versions of the Kemp adaptation as it developed in performance from 1948 to 1959. The ending of the Lord Chamberlain's restrictive practices has allowed the re-instatement of lines cut from the original Festival production. Some cuts made for artistic reasons in subsequent productions are retained, and several additions which worked well in Guthrie's last production are likewise kept. There are one or two minor alterations where I have felt that Lyndsay's original intent was being obscured by the transfer of a speech from one character to another. A song written by myself and based on a poem by Robert Henryson, has been added to Part Two.

Tom Fleming.

THE EDINBURGH INTERNATIONAL FESTIVAL PRODUCTION
Assembly Hall 12 August-1 September 1984
CAST

DILIGENCE, a herald	Tom Watson
KING HUMANITIE	David Rintoul
WANTONNESS	Paul Young
PLACEBO three courtiers	John Buick
SOLACE	Tony Roper
DAME SENSUALITIE	Caroline Kaart
HAMELINESS her handmaids	Gerda Stevenson
DANGER	Fiona Kennedy
FUND-JENNET, a porter	Halcro Johnston
GUDE COUNSEL	Alex McAvoy
FLATTERIE	Walter Carr
FALSEHOOD three Vices	Gregor Fisher
DECEIT	John Grieve
SOUTAR, a cobbler	Ian Stewart
TAILOR	Robert Trotter
SOUTAR'S WIFE	Tricia Scott
TAILOR'S WIFE	Kay Gallie
SPIRITUALITIE, a bishop	Roy Hanlon
PRIORESS	Juliet Cadzow
ABBOT	Andrew Cruickshank
PARSON	Alexander West
TEMPORALITIE, a Lord	John Shedden
MERCHANT	Brown Derby
CORRECTION'S VARLET	Colin Gourley
DIVINE CORRECTION	Robert Urquhart
POOR MAN	Phil McCall
PARDONER	Walter Carr
WILKIN WIDDIEFOW, his boy	Ian Briggs
JOHN THE COMMON-WEAL	Alec Heggie
A SERGEANT	Bill Riddoch
A SCRIBE	John Cobb
A SWORDBEARER	David Monteath
A BOY	Ranald Neilson

THE THRIE ESTAITES, THE PEOPLE, SOLDIERS.

Director TOM FLEMING	Designer NADINE BAYLIS
Lighting ANDRÉ TAMMES	Musical Director JOHN GRUNDY

ANE SATYRE OF THE THRIE ESTAITES

FIRST PART

ESTAITES

(A fanfare of trumpets)
(singing)
The Father, founder of faith and felicitie,
That your fashion formit to his similitude;
And his Son, our Saviour, shield in necessitie,
That bocht you from bane, ransomed on the Rood,
Re-pledging his prisoners with his heart-blude;
The Haly Ghaist, governor and grounder of grace,
Of wisdom and welfare baith fountain and flood,
Save you all that we see seated in this place,
         And shield you from sin,
And with his Spirit you inspire
Till we have shown our desire!
Silence, Sovereigns, we require,
         For now we begin!

*(During the singing, DILIGENCE
a herald, and the THRIE
ESTAITES enter)*

DILIGENCE

People, tak tent to me, and hold you coy![1]
Here am I sent to you, ane messenger,
From ane noble and richt redoubtit Roy,[2]
The whilk has been absent this mony a year,
Wha bade me show to you, but[3] variance,
That he intends amang you to appear,
With ane triumphant awful ordinance,
With crown and sword and sceptre in his hand,
Temperit with mercy when penitence appears;
Howbeit that he lang time has been sleepand,[4]
Wherethrow misrule has reigned thir mony years
And innocents been brocht upon their biers
By false reporters of this nation . . .
Though young oppressors at their elders leirs,[5]
Be now weel sure of reformation!

(Fanfare)

And here by open proclamation
I warn in name of his magnificence,
The Thrie Estaites of this nation,
That they compear with debtful diligence.
And till his grace make their obedience.
And first I warn the Spiritualitie,

---

[1]quiet   [2]king   [3]without   [4]sleeping   [5]learns

DILIGENCE
(Contd)

And see the Burgesses spare nocht for expense,
But speed them here with Temporalitie.
(As DILIGENCE *names them,*
SPIRITUALITIE,
TEMPORALITIE,
the BURGESSES *and their*
respective trains stand.
DILIGENCE *turns to the*
audience again)

And I beseek you, famous auditors,
Convenit into this congregation
To be patient the space of certain hours
Till ye have heard our short narration.
Also we make you supplication
That no man tak our words intill disdain,
Howbeit ye hear by lamentation,
The Common-Weal richt piteously complain.

Prudent people, I pray you all,
Tak no man grief in speciall:
For we sall speak in general,
                For pastime and for play.
Therefore, till all our rhymes be rung,
And our mis-tonit sangs be sung,
Let every man keep weel ane tongue . . .
                And every woman twae!

(A Fanfare and March.
KING HUMANITIE *enters with his*
train. DILIGENCE *moves*
aside)

KING

O Lord of lords, and King of kingës all,
Omnipotent of power, Prince but peer,
Eternal reignand in gloire celestial,
Unmade Makar, whilk, havand no matter,
Made heaven and earth, fire, air and water clear
Send me thy grace with peace perpetual,
That I may rule my realm to thy plaisir;
Syne bring my saul to joy angelical.

I thee request, wha rent was on the Rood,
Me to defend from deedës of defame,
That my people report of me but gude,
And be my safegaird baith from sin and shame.
I know my days endures but as a dream;
Therefore, O Lord, heartly I thee exhort
To give me grace to use my diadem
To thy pleasure and to my great comfort.

ESTAITES	Amen: Amen: Amen.
SONG	To Thee psalms will I sing Nor in the floral ring Wi' ladies cleir Persue the galliard's round While shawms by jocund sound Owreset my (his) ear.
	Cinquepace[1] and proud pavane Maun yield to the hosan; Beauty is fair But ane anointit King His dolent psalms maun sing For evermair.
	(*The* KING *takes his seat upon his throne.* WANTONNESS *enters, with* PLACEBO *at his heels*)

WANTONNESS	My Sovereign Lord and Prince but peer,
	What gars you mak sic dreary cheer?
	Be blithe sae lang as ye are here,
	          And pass time with pleasure:
	For as lang lives the merry man
	As the sorry, for ocht he can.
	His banes full sair, Sir, sall I ban[2]
	          That daes you displeasure.
	Sae lang as Placebo and I
	Remains into your company,
	Your grace sall live richt merrily,
	          Of this have ye nae doubt.
	Sae lang as ye have us in cure,
	Your grace, Sir, sall want nae pleasure:
	Were Solace here, I you assure,
	          He wad rejoice this rout!

PLACEBO	Gude brother mine, where is Solace,
	The mirror of all merriness?
	I have great marvel, by the Mass
	          He's tarryan' sae lang.
	Bide he awa, we are but shent![3]
	I ferly[4] how he frae us went.
	I trow he has impediment
	          That lets him nocht to gang.

WANTONNESS	I left Solace, that same great loon, Drinkand into the burgh's toun — It will cost him half ane croun Although he had nae mair.

[1]a lively dance   [2]curse   [3]lost   [4]wonder

WANTONNESS (Contd)	Also, he said he wad gang see Fair Lady Sensualitie, The beriall of all beauty, And portraiture preclair.

(Enter SOLACE *running)*

PLACEBO	By God, I see him at the last, As he were chased, rinnan' richt fast; He glowers, even as he were aghast, Or fleyit of ane ghaist . . .
SOLACE	*(Drunk, at first to audience)*

Wow! Wha saw ever sic a thrang?
Me thocht some said I had gane wrang.
Had I help, I wad sing ane sang
         With a richt merry noise!
I have sic pleasure at my heart
That gars me sing the treble part —
Wad some gude fellow fill the quart
         That wad my heart rejoice?
What is my name? Can ye not guess?
Sirs, ken ye not Sandy Solace?
They callit my mother Bonny Bess
         That dwelt between the Bows.
At twelve year auld she learnit to swyve,[1]
Thankit be thee, great God of life,
She made me fathers four or five —
         But doubt, this isna mowse![2]
And if I lie, sirs, ye may speir.
But saw ye not the King come here?
I am ane sporter and play-fere[3]
         To that young King.
He said he wad, within short space,
To pass his time, come to this place —

KING	My servant Solace.
SOLACE	I pray to God to give him grace And lang to reign.
KING	What gart you tarry?

SOLACE	I wat[4]not, sir, by sweet Saint Mary;
	I have been in a fairy-fairy
	         Or else intill a trance.
	Sir, I have seen, I you assure,
	The fairest earthly creature,
	That ever was formit by nature
	         And maist for to advance.

---

[1]have sex   [2]commonplace   [3]mate   [4]know

To look on her is great delyte,
With lippës reid and cheekës white,
I wad renounce all this warld quite
          To stand intill her grace!
She is wanton and she is wise,
And clad she is in the new guise —
It wad gar all your flesh up-rise
          To look upon her face
Were I a king, it should be kend,
I should not spare on her to spend
And this same nicht for her to send
          For my pleasure!
What rack of your prosperity,
Gif ye want Sensualitie?
I wad not give a silly flee
          For your treasure!

KING
    Forsooth, my friends, I think ye are not wise,
To counsel me to break commandëment
Directit by the Prince of Paradise;
Considering ye knaw that mine intent
Is for to be til God obedient,
Wha does forbid men to be lecherous.
Do I not so, perchance I sall repent.
Therefore I think your counsel odious.
          The whilk ye gave me til
Because I have been to this day
Tanquam tabula rasa[1]
          Ready for gude and ill.

PLACEBO
    Believe ye that we will beguile you?
Or from your virtue we will wile you?
Or with our evil counsel file you,
          Both into gude and evil?
To tak your grace's part we grant,
In all your deeds participant,
Sae that ye be not a young saint
          And syne an auld devil.

WANTONNESS
    Believe ye, sir, that lechery be sin?
Na, trow nocht that! This is my reason why.
First at the Roman Court will ye begin,
Whilk is the lemand lamp of lechery,
Where cardinals and bishops generally
To love ladies they think a pleasant sport.
And out of Rome has banished Chastitie,
Wha with our prelates can get nae resort!

SOLACE
    Sir, till you get a prudent queen,

[1] like a tablet without writing

SOLACE
(Contd)
	I think your Majesty serene
	Should have ane lusty concubine
	        To play you with all;
	For I know, by your quality,
	Ye want the gift of chastity.
	Fall to, *in nomine Domini!*
	        For this is my counsel!
	I speak, sir, under protestation
	That none at me have indignation,
	For all the prelates of this nation
	        For the maist part,
	They think nae shame to have a hure
	And some has three under their cure —
	This to be true I'll you assure,
	        Ye sall hear afterwart.
	Sir, knew ye all the matter throw[1]
	        To play ye wad begin.
	Speir at the Monks of Balmerino
	        Gif lechery be sin!

PLACEBO	Sir, send forth Sandy Solace,
	Or else your minion Wantonness
	And pray my Lady Prioress
	        The sooth[2] to declare,
	Gif it be sin to tak a Katie
	Or to live like a Bummillbaty.[3]
	The Book says *"Omnia probate"*[4]
	        And nocht for to spare!

WANTONNESS	Come this way, sir, I'll speak you clear; A word, sir, in your royal ear, List you to me, your ain playfere, For time is runnan' past.
PLACEBO	Good physic, sir, he has for you! Away, sir, it were best you knew What Wantonness now wills you do — The lady's coman' fast. (LADY SENSUALITIE *enters,* *accompanied by her maidens* HAMELINESS *and* DANGER, *and by* FUND-JENNET. *They take* *up their position on a part of* *the stage distant from the* KING, *who does not see them*)
SENSUALITIE	Lovers, awake! Behauld the fiery sphere,

---

[1]through   [2]truth   [3]booby   [4]"Try everything"

Behauld the natural dochter of Venus!
Behauld, lovers, this lusty lady clear,
The fresh fountain of knichtës amorous,
Replete with joys, douce and delicious!
Or wha wad mak to Venus observance
In my mirth-full chalmer melodious,
There sall they find all pastime and pleasance.

Behauld my heid, behauld my gay attire,
Behauld my halse[1] lovesome and lily-white;
Behauld my visage flammand as the fire,
Behauld my paps, of portraiture perfyte!

SENSUALITIE (Contd)
To look on me lovers has great delyte;
Richt so has all the kings of Christendom —
To them I have done pleasures infinite
And specially unto the Court of Rome.

Ane kiss of me were worth, in ane morning,
A milliön of gold to knicht or king.
And yet I am of nature so towart
I let no lover pass with ane sair heart.
Of my name, wad ye wit the verity?
Forsooth they call me Sensualitie.
I haud it best now, ere we farther gang,
To dame Venus let us go sing a sang.

HAMELINESS
Madame, but tarrying,
For to serve Venus dear
We sall fall to and sing.
Sister Danger, come near!

DANGER
Sister, sing this sang I may not,
Without the help of gude Fund-Jennet,
Fund-Jennet, ho! Come tak a part!

FUND-JENNET
That sall I do with all my heart!
Sister, howbeit that I am hairse,
I am content to bear a bass.
Ye twa should love me as your life —
Ye knaw I learnit you baith to swyve
In my chalmer, ye wat weel where,
Sin syne the feind a man ye spare!

HAMELINESS
Fund-Jennet, fie, ye are to blame!
To speak foul words think ye not shame?

FUND-JENNET
There is a hunder here sittan' by,
That loves japing as well as I,
Micht they get it in privitie —
But wha begins the sang, let see!

[1]neck

FUND-JENNET
(Contd)

*(Song. Verses from the poem
by Alexander Montgomerie
b.1545)*

Hey nou the day daws,
The jolly cock craws,
Nou shroudës the shaws[1]
      Throu Nature anon.
The Thissell-cock crys
On lovers wha lies,
Now skailës[2] the skys,
      The nicht is near gone!

ALL WOMEN

(singing)
The fields overflows,
With gowans that grows,
Where lilies like lowe[1] is,
      As reid as the roan[2]:
The turtle that true is
With notes that renews,
Her party pursues
      The nicht is near gone!

Now hartës with hinds
Conform to their kinds
High turses their tynds,[5]
      On ground where they groan,
Now urcheons,[6] with hairs,
Aye passes in pairs,
Whilk duly declares
      The nicht is near gone.

*(During the singing of the
song the* KING *has pricked
up his ears. He rouses*
WANTONNESS, *who has fallen
asleep)*

KING

Methocht I heard ane merry sang.
Up, Wantonness, thou sleeps too lang!
I thee command in haste to gang,
See what yon mirth may mean!

WANTONNESS

I trow, sir, by the Trinity,
Yon same is Sensualitie,
Gif it be so, soon sall I see
      That sovereign serene!

PLACEBO

(In his ear)
Sir, she is meikle to advance,
For she can baith play and dance,

---

[1]woods [2]empties [3]flame [4]rowan [5]tosses their antlers [6]hedge-hogs

That perfyte patron of pleasance,
                    Ane pearl of pulchritude!
Saft as the silk is her white lyre[1]
Her hair is like the golden wire,
My heart burns in a flame of fire
                    I swear you by the Rood!

SOLACE   *(In the other ear)*
What say ye, sir? Are ye content
That she come here incontinent?[2]
What vails your kingdom and your rent
                    And all your great treasure,
Without you have ane merry life,
And cast aside all sturt and strife?
And sae lang as ye want a wife,
                    Fall to, and tak your pleasure!

KING   Forsooth, I wat not how it stands,
But since I heard of your tidands,
My bodie trembles, feet and hands,
                    And whiles is haet as fire!
I trow Cupido with his dart
Has woundit me out-throw the heart;
My spreit will frae my body part,
                    Get I nocht my desire
Pass on, away, with diligence,
And bring her here to my presence!
Spare nocht for travel nor expense,
                    I care not for nae cost!
Pass on your way soon, Wantonness,
And tak with you Sandy Solace,
And bring that Lady to this place,
                    Or else I am but lost!
Commend me to that sweetest thing,
Present her with this same rich ring,
And say I lie in languishing,
                    Except she mak remeid!
With sighing sair I am but shent,
Without she come incontinent
My heavy langour to relent
                    And save me now frae deid![3]

WANTONNESS   Doubt ye not, sir, but we will get her,
We sall be fiery for to fet[4] her,
But, faith, we wad speed all the better
                    Had I mair than a plack![5]

[1]skin   [2]without delay   [3]death   [4]fetch   [5]halfpenny

SOLACE | (WANTONNESS *holds purse*
upside down to point meaning)

SOLACE

Sir, let-na sorrow in you sink,
But give us ducats for a drink
And we sall never sleep a wink
       Till we have brocht her back!

(The KING *gives them purses)*

KING

I pray you, speed you soon again!

WANTONNESS

Yea, of this sang, sir, we are fain!
We sall neither spare for wind nor rain
       Till our day's wark be done!
Fareweel, for we are at the flicht!
Placebo, rule our Roy at richt —
We sall be here, man, ere midnicht
       Though we march with the moon!

(A joyous march. SOLACE *and*
WANTONNESS *make a detour of*
the stage and come to
SENSUALITIE *and her court)*

WANTONNESS

Pastime with pleasance and great prosperity
Be to you, Sovereign Sensualitie!

SENSUALITIE

Sirs, ye are welcome. Where go ye?
East or West?

WANTONNESS

In faith, I trow we be at the farrest!

SENSUALITIE

What is your name? I pray you, sir, declare!

WANTONNESS

Marry, Wantonness, the King's secretair.

SENSUALITIE

What king is that, whilk has sae gay a boy?

WANTONNESS

Humanitie, that rich redoubtit Roy
Wha does commend him to you heart-fully,
And sends you here a ring with ane ruby,
In token that above all creäture
He has chosen you to be his Paramour:
He bade me say that he will be but deid,
Without that ye mak hastily remeid.

SENSUALITIE

How can I help him, though she should for-fare?[1]
Ye ken richt weel I'm nae Medicinar.

SOLACE

Ane kiss of your sweet mou, in ane morning,
Till his sickness micht be great comforting.
Also he maks you supplication
This nicht to mak with him collation.

SENSUALITIE

I thank his grace of his benevolence!

[1]die

Gude sirs, I sall be ready even frae-hand.
In me there sall be found nae negligence,
Baith day and nicht, when his grace will demand.
Pass ye before, and say I am comand.[1]
And thinks richt lang to have of him ané sicht.
And I to Venus mak ane faithful band
That in his arms I think to lie all nicht.

WANTONNESS   That sall be done . . . but yet or I hame pass,
Here I protest for Hameliness, your lass.

SENSUALITIE   She sall be at command, sir, when ye will;
I trust she sall you find flinging your fill!

WANTONNESS   Now hey for joy and mirth I dance!
Tak there ane gay gamond of France

*(A dance, on a French rhythm
— a "gamond".*
WANTONNESS *and* SOLACE
dance their way back towards
KING)

WANTONNESS   Gude morrow, Maister, by the Mess

KING   Welcome, my minion Wantonness!
How has thou sped in thy travel?

WANTONNESS   Richt weel, by him that herryit hell!
Your errand is weel done!

KING   *(In a transport)*
Then, Wantonness, full weel is me!
Thou has deservit baith meat and fee,
By Him that made the moon!
(Anxiously)
There is ane thing that I wad speir . . . .
What sall do when she comes here?
For I know nocht the craft perqueir[2]
Of lovers' gin,[3]
Therefore at length ye maun me leir
How to begin.

WANTONNESS   To kiss and clap her, sir, be not affeared!
She will not shrink though you kiss her a span
within the beard.
Gif ye think she thinks shame, then hide the
bairn's heid
With her train, and tent her weel, ye wat
what I mean!
Will ye give me leave, sir, first to go to,
And I sall learn you the cues how ye sall do?

[1]coming [2]by heart [3]skill

KING	God forbid, Wantonness, that I give thee leave!
	Thou art owre perilous ane page sic practicks
	<div align="right">to preeve[3]!</div>

(WANTONNESS *spies*
SENSUALITIE)

WANTONNESS	Now, sir, preeve as ye please, I see her comand!
	Order you with gravity, we sall by you stand!

(*The* KING *and his
courtiers prepare to welcome*
SENSUALITIE.
SENSUALITIE, *apart, first
takes her vow to Venus*)

SENSUALITIE	O Venus goddess, unto thy celsitude
	I give laud, gloire, honour, and reverence,
	Whilk grantit me sic perfyte pulchritude,
	That princes of my person have pleasance,
	I make ane vow, with humble observance,
	That I will in thy temple visit thee
	With sacrifice unto thy deity!

(*She turns towards the* KING)

SENSUALITIE (Contd)	And now my way I maun advance
	Unto ane prince of great puissance,
	Whilk young men has in governance,
	<div align="right">Rolland into his rage.</div>
	I am richt glad, I you assure,
	That potent prince to get in cure,
	Wha is of lustiness the lure
	<div align="right">And greatest of courage.</div>
	O potent prince, of pulchritude preclair,
	God Cupido preserve your celsitude!
	May the dame Venus keep your court from care,
	As I wad she should keep my ain heart-blude!

KING	Welcome to me peerless of pulchritude!
	Welcome to me, thou sweeter than the amber,
	Wha may of all my dolour me denude! . . .
	Solace, convoy this lady to my chamber!

SENSUALITIE	I gang this gait with richt gude will.
	Sir Wantonness, tarry ye still?
	And, Hameliness, the cup ye's fill
	<div align="right">And bear him company!</div>

HAMELINESS	That sall I do, withouten doubt,
	For he and I sall play cap-out!

[1]try

	(KING, SENSUALITIE, SOLACE, PLACEBO *and* DANGER, *retire followed by* WANTONNESS *and* HAMELINESS)
WANTONNESS	*(taking a cup from her)* Your Dame, by now truly, Has gotten upon her keel! What rack though ye and I Go join the joust as weel?
HAMELINESS	Content I am with richt gude will, Whenever ye are ready, All your pleasure to fulfil!

WANTONNESS	Now, weel said, by our Lady!
	I'll bear my master company,
	      As lang as I endure!
	If he be whiskand wantonly,
	      We sall fling on the floor!

GUDE COUNSEL	Consider, my sovereigns, I you beseek,
	The cause maist principal of my coming.
	Princes or potestates are not worth a leek,
	Be they not guided by my gude governing.
	There was never emperor, conqueror, nor king,
	Without my wisdom that micht their weal advance.
	My name is Gude Counsel, without feigning;
	Lords for lack of my law are brocht to mischance.
	And so, for conclusion,
	Wha guides them not by Gude Counsel,
	All in vain is their travail,
	And finally fortune sall them fail,
	And bring them to confusion.
	      And this I understand,
	For I have my residence
	With high princes of great puissance
	In England, Italy and France,
	      And mony other land,
	But out of Scotland, alas,
	I have been banished lang space —
	That gars our rulers all want grace,
	      And die before their day!
	Because they lichtlyt[1] Gude Counsel,
	Fortune turnit on them her sail,
	Whilk brocht this realm to meikle bale —
	      Wha can the contrair say?
	My lords, I cam not here to lie;
	Waes me for King Humanitie,

[1]made light of

GUDE COUNSEL
(Contd)
	Owreset with Sensualitie
	       In his first beginning,
	Throw vicious counsel insolent!
	So they may get riches or rent
	To his weilfare they tak nae tent,
	       Nor what sall be the ending!
	But wad the King be guided yet with reason
	And on mis-doers mak punition,
	Howbeit that I lang time have been exilit
	I traist in God my name sall yet be stylit,
	So till I see God send mair of his grace,
	I purpose till repose me in this place.

(GUDE COUNSEL
*draws apart, as
enter* FLATTERIE *boisterously*)

FLATTERIE	Mak room, sirs ho! that I may rin.
	Lo, see how I am new come in,
	       Begariet all with sundry hues!
	Let be your din till I begin,
	       And I sall show you of my news!
	Throwout all Christendom I have past
	And am come here now at the last,
	       Stormstayed on sea aye sen Yule day,
	That we were fain to hew our mast,
	       Not half a mile beyond the May.
	But now amang you I will remain,
	I purpose never to sail again,
	       To put my life in chance of watter.
	Was never seen sic wind and rain,
	       Nor of shipmen sic clitter-clatter.
	Some bade "Hail!" and some bade "Stand-by!"
	"On starboard ho!" "A-luff, fie fie!"
	       Till all the rapes began to rattle,
	Was never wight sae fley't[1] as I,
	       When all the sails played brittle-brattle!
	To see the waves, it was a wonder,
	And wind, that rave the sails in sinder!
	Now am I scapit frae that affray;
	What say ye, sirs, am I not gay?
	       Ken ye not Flatterie, your ain fule
	That gaed to mak this new array?
	       Was I not here with you at Yule!
	Yes, by my faith, I think on weel!
	Where are my fellows that wad not fail?
	We should have come here for a cast!
	Ho, Falsehood, ho!

[1]scared

	(FALSEHOOD enters)
FALSEHOOD	We serve the Deil! Wha's that that cries for me sae fast?
FLATTERIE	Why, Falsehood, brother, knaws thou not me? I am thy brother, Flatterie!
FALSEHOOD	Now let me brace thee in my arms, When friend meets friend, the heart aye warms!
FLATTERIE	Where is Deceit, that limmer loon?
FALSEHOOD	I left him drinkand in the toun; He will be here incontinent.
FLATTERIE	Now by the Haly Sacrament, Thae tidings comforts all my heart! He is richt crafty as ye ken, And counsellor to the Merchant-men!
	(Enter DECEIT*)*

DECEIT	Bon jour, brother, with all my heart,
	Here am I come to tak your part
	               Baith into gude and evil!
	I met Gude Counsel by the way,
	Wha pat me in a felon fray[1]
	               I gave him to the devil!
	How come ye here, I pray you tell me!

FALSEHOOD	Marry, to seek King Humanitie!
DECEIT	Now, by the gude lady that me bare, That same horse is my ain mare! Sen we three seeks yon noble King, Let us devise some subtle thing! Also, I pray you as your brother, That we, ilk ane, be true to other. I pray to God, nor I be hangit, But I sall die ere ye be wrangit!
FALSEHOOD	What is thy counsel that we do?
DECEIT	Marry, sirs this is my counsel, lo! Frae time the King begin to stir him, I dreid Gude Counsel may come near him. And be we known to Lord Correction, It will be our confusion. Therefore, my dear brother, devise To find some toy of the new guise.
FLATTERIE	Marry, I sall find a thousand wiles. We maun turn our claiths, and change our styles, And disaguise us, that nae man ken us.

[1]terrible fear

FLATTERIE (Contd)	Has nae men clerk's claithing to lend us? And let us keep grave countenance, As we were new come out of France!
DECEIT	Now, by my saul, that is weel devysit! Ye sall see me soon disagysit.
FALSEHOOD	And sae sall I, man, by the Rood! Now, some gude fellow, lend me a hood! (FLATTERIE *helps* DECEIT *and* FALSEHOOD *to disguise* *themselves*)
DECEIT	Now am I buskit, and wha can spy? The devil stick me, if this be I! If this be I, or not, I cannot weel say, Or has the Fiend of Fairy-folk borne me away?
FALSEHOOD	What says thou of my gay garmoun?[1]
DECEIT	I say thou looks even like a loon. Now, brother Flatterie, what do ye? What kind of man shape ye to be?
FLATTERIE	Now, by my faith, my brother dear, I will gang counterfeit a Friar!
DECEIT	A friar? Whereto? Ye cannot preach?
FLATTERIE	What rack, if I can flatter and fleech? Perchance I'll come to that honour, To be the kingës confessor. Puir friars are free at ony feast, And marshallit aye amang the best! (DECEIT *has fetched* *a monk's cowl, and shaves a* *tonsure on* FLATTERIE'S *head*)
DECEIT	Here is thy gaining, all and some, That is a cowl of Tullilum!
FLATTERIE	Wha has a breviary to lend me? The fiend a saul I trow will ken me!
FALSEHOOD	We maun do mair yet, by Saint James! For we maun all three change our names. Christen me, and I sall baptise thee. (*There follows a mock* *ceremony*)
DECEIT	By God and thereabout may it be! How will thou call me, I pray thee tell?
FALSEHOOD	I wat not how to call mysel!

DECEIT	But yet aince name the bairnie's name!
FALSEHOOD	Discretion, Discretion in God's name!
DECEIT	I need not now to care for thrift, But what sall be my Godbairn gift?
FALSEHOOD	I give you all the devils of hell!
DECEIT	No, brother, hauld that to thysel! Now, sit doun! Let me baptise thee — I wat na what thy name should be.
FALSEHOOD	But yet aince name the bairn's name!
DECEIT	Sapience, Sapience, in God's name!
FLATTERIE	Brother Deceit, come baptise me.
DECEIT	Then sit down lowly on thy knee!
FLATTERIE	Now, brother, name the bairn's name.
DECEIT	Devotion, in the devil's name. (*He splashes* FLATTERIE)
FLATTERIE	The deil receive thee, lurdan loon! Thou has wet all my new shaven croun!
DECEIT	Devotion, Sapience and Discretion — We three may rule this region. We sall find mony crafty things For to beguile a hundred kings! For thou (*to* FALSEHOOD) can richt weel crack and clatter. And I sall feign, and thou (*to* FLATTERIE) sall flatter.
FLATTERIE	But I wad have, ere we depairtit, A drink to mak us better heartit.
DECEIT	Weel said, by Him that herryit hell, I was even thinkan' that mysel! (*While the* THREE VICES *are drinking, the* KING *appears leading* SENSUALITIE *from the gallery*)
KING	Now, where is Placebo and Solace? Where is my minion Wantonness? Wantonness, ho! Come to me soon! (WANTONNESS *appears from the gallery with clothes some- what disordered, with* HAMELI- NESS)
WANTONNESS	Why cryit, ye, sir, till I had done!
KING	What was ye dae'an, tell me that?

WANTONNESS	Marry, learand how my faither me gat! I wat not how it stands; but doubt Me think the warld rins round about!
KING	And sae think I, man, by my thrift! I see fifteen moons in the lift.[1]
	(*Enter* SOLACE *and* PLACEBO *with* DANGER, *from the gallery*)
SOLACE	Now show me, sir, I you exhort, How are ye of your love content? Think ye not this a merry sport?
KING	Yea, that I do in verament![2]
	(*The* KING *spies the* THREE VICES)
	What bairns are yon upon the bent? I did not see them all this day.
WANTONNESS	They will be here incontinent. Stand still and hear what they will say.
	(*The* THREE VICES *come* *forward and salute the* KING)
DECEIT	Laud, honour, gloire, triumph and victory . . .
FLATTERIE	Be to your maist excellent Majesty!
KING	Ye are welcome, gude friends, by the Rood! Apparently ye seem some men of gude. What are your names, tell me without delay!
DECEIT	Discretion, Sir, is my name perfay.
KING	What is your name, sir, with the clippit croun?
FLATTERIE	But doubt my name is callit Devotion.
KING	Welcome, Devotion, by Saint Jame! Now sirrah, tell what is your name?
FALSEHOOD	Marry, sir, they call me . . . what call they me? (*Aside*) I wat not weel, but gif I lie!
KING	Can ye not tell what is your name?
FALSEHOOD	I kennd it when I cam frae hame!
KING	What ails ye cannot show it now?
FALSEHOOD	(*rattled*) Marry, they call me Thin-Drink, I trow!
KING	Thin-Drink? What kind of name is that?
DECEIT	(*whispers*) Sapience! Thou serves to bear a plate! Methinks thou shows thee not weel-wittit.

[1]sky [2]truth

FALSEHOOD	Sypeins[1], sir, Sypeins, marry now ye hit it!
FLATTERIE	(*shutting* FALSEHOOD *up with a gesture*) Sir, if ye please to let me say, His name is Sapientia!
FALSEHOOD	That name is it, by Saint Michael!
KING	Why could thou not tell it thysel?
FALSEHOOD	I pray your grace to pardon me. And I sall show the veritie! I am sae full of Sapience, That some-time I will take ane trance! My spreit was reft frae my body, Noo, heich abune the Trinity.
KING	Sapience should be a man of gude.
FALSEHOOD	Sir, ye may ken that by my hood!
KING	Now have I Sapience and Discretion, How can I fail to rule this region? And Devotion to be my confessor! Thir three came in ane happy hour! Here I mak thee my secretar, (*to* FALSEHOOD) And thou sall be my treasurer (*to* DECEIT) And thou sall be my counsellor In spiritual things, and confessor (*to* FLATTERIE).

FLATTERIE	I swear to you, sir, by Saint Ann,
	Ye never met a wiser man,
	For mony a craft, sir, do I can,
	        Were they weel knawn;
	I have nae feel of flattery,
	But fosterit with philosophy,
	A strang man in astronomy,
	        Whilk sall be soon shawn!

FALSEHOOD	And I have great intelligence,
	In quelling of the quintessence[2]
	But to preeve my experience,
	        Sir, lend me forty crouns!
	To mak multiplication.
	And tak my obligation —
	Gif we make false narration.
	        Hold us for very loons!

DECEIT	Sir I ken by your physnomie, Ye sall conquer, or else I lie, Danskin,[3] Denmark, and Almane, Spitalfield and the Realm of Spain. You sall have at your governance

[1]weak ale i.e. Thin-Drink   [2]alchemy relating to heavenly bodies   [3]Danzig

DECEIT (Contd)	Renfrew and the Realm of France, Yea, Ruglen and the toun of Rome, Corstorphine and all Christendom. Whereto, sir, by the Trinity, Ye are ane very *A per se!*
FLATTERIE	Sir, when I dwelt in Italy, I leirit the craft of palmistry. Shaw me the loof[1], sir, of your hand, And I sall gar you understand If your grace be unfortunate Of if ye be predestinate. (KING *shows hand*) I see ye will have fifteen queens And fifteen score of concubines! The Virgin Mary save your grace, Saw ever man sae white a face, Sae great ane arm, sae fair ane hand, Or sic a leg in all this land! Were ye in arms, I think nae wonder, Howbeit ye dang doun fifteen hunder
KING	Ye are richt welcome, by the Rood! Ye seem to be three men of gude! (*He sees* GUDE COUNSEL *who comes forward*) But wha is yon that stands sae still? Gae spy and speir what is his will. And if he yearns of my presence, Bring him to me with diligence. (KING *sits with* SENSUALITIE. *The* THREE VICES *quickly confer*)
FLATTERIE	I doubt full sair by God Himsel That yon auld carl be Gude Counsel! Get he aince to the King's presence, We three will get nae audience!
DECEIT	That matter I sall tak on hand, And say it is the King's command, That he anon avoid this place, And come not near the Kingës grace, And that under the pain of treason!
FLATTERIE	Brother, I hold your counsel reason. Now let us hear what he will say. (*Addressing* GUDE COUNSEL)

[1]palm

	Auld lyart beard, gude day, gude day!
GUDE COUNSEL	Gude day again, sirs, by the Rood! I pray God mak you men of gude!
DECEIT	Pray not for us to Lord nor Lady. For we are men of gude already! Sir, show to us what is your name?
GUDE COUNSEL	Gude Counsel they call me at hame.
FALSEHOOD	What says thou, carle, art thou Gude Counsel? Swift, pack thee hence, unhappy mortal!
GUDE COUNSEL	I pray you, sirs, give me licence, To come aince to the King's presence To speak but twa words to his grace.
FLATTERIE	Quick, hure-son carle, devoid this place!
GUDE COUNSEL	Brother, I ken you weel eneuch, Howbeit ye mak it never sae teuch — Flatterie, Deceit and False-Report That will not suffer to resort Gude Counsel to the King's presence.
DECEIT	Swith, hure-soon carle, gang pack thee hence! If ever thou come this gait again, I vow to God, thou shall be slain!

(*They hurl* GUDE COUNSEL *away*)

GUDE COUNSEL	Sen at this time I can get nae presence, Is nae remeid but bide in patience. (*Looking at* KING) But when youth-heid has blawn his wanton blast, Then sall Gude Counsel rule him at the last!

(*Exit* GUDE COUNSEL. *The*
THREE VICES *return to the* KING)

KING	What gart you bide sae lang frae my presence? I think it lang since ye departit thence. What was yon man, with ane great boustious[1] beard? Me thocht he made you all three very feard!
DECEIT	It was a laithsome lurdan loun, Come to break booths into this toun! We have gart bind him with a pole, And send him to the Thievës' Hole.
KING	Let him sit there with ane mischance! And let us go to our pastimes.
WANTONNESS	Better go revel at the racket, Or else go to the hurly-hacket, Or then to show our courtly courses,

[1]rough

WANTONNESS (Contd)	Gae see wha best can rin their horses!

(As they make to move,
SOLACE *stops them)*

SOLACE Na, Sovereign, ere we farther gang.
Gar Sensualitie sing ane sang.

(The LADIES *sing a song,*
and the THE KING *lies down*
among them)

(Song. Verses from poem by
Alexander Scott b.1520)

To love unlovit is ane pane,
For she that is my soverane
   Some wanton man so he has set her
That I can get no love again,
    But breaks my heart, and nocht the better.

Whattan ane glaikit[1] fule am I,
To slay myself with melancholy,
   Sen weel I ken I may nocht get her!
Or what should be the cause, and why,
    To break my heart and nocht the better?

My heart, sen thou may nocht her please,
Adieu! as gude love comes as gaes!
   Go choose another and forget her!
God give him dolour and disease
    That breaks their heart, and nocht the better.

(As the song ends, VERITIE *enters,*
holding Book, i.e. HOLY BIBLE.
She stands apart, but
FLATTERIE *goes out to*
peer at her as she speaks)

VERITIE *(To audience)*
Gif men of me wad have intelligence,
Or knaw my name, they call me Veritie.
Of Christës law I have experience,
And have owre-sailit mony a stormy sea.
Now am I seekan' King Humanitie;
For of his grace I have gude esperance.
Fra time that he acquaintit be with me,
His honour and heich gloire I sall advance.

(As FLATTERIE *returns* DECEIT
greets him).

DECEIT Gude day, Father, where have ye been?

---

[1]simple

	Declare till us of your novelles.
FLATTERIE	There is now lichtit on the green, Dame Veritie, by books and bells! But come she to the King's presence, There is nae boot for us to bide! Therefore I rede us, all go hence!
FALSEHOOD	That will be not yet, by Saint Bride! But we sall either gang or ride To Lords of Spiritualitie, And gar them trow yon bag of pride Has spoken manifest heresy!
FLATTERIE	O reverent fathers of the Spiritual State, We counsel you be wise and vigilant! Dame Veritie has lichtit now of late, And in her hand bearand the New Testament!
SPIRITUALITIE	I haud it best that we incontinent Gar haud her fast into captivity, Unto the thrid day of the Parliament And then accuse her of her heresy.

(The THREE VICES *approach*
VERITIE)

FLATTERIE	What buik is that, harlot, in thy hand?

(He looks at it)

	Out! Waylaway! This is the New Testament, In English tongue, and prentit in England! Heresy, heresy! Fire, fire incontinent!
VERITIE	Forsooth, my friend, ye have ane wrang judgement, For in this Buik there is nae heresy, But our Christ's word, richt douce and redolent — Ane springand well of sincere verity!
DECEIT	Come on your way, for all your yellow locks! Your wanton words but doubt ye sall repent! This nicht ye sall forfare[1] ane pair of stocks, And syne the morn be brocht to thole[2] judgement.

*(VERITIE falls on her knees,
not to the VICES, but
to HEAVEN)*

VERITIE	Get up, thou sleepës all too lang, O Lord, And mak some reasonable reformation On them that does tramp doun thy gracious word, And has ane deidly indignation At them wha maks the true narration!

---

[1]endure [2]suffer

FLATTERIE	Sit doun and tak you rest, All nicht till it be day!
	(*They put* VERITIE *in the stocks and return to* SPIRITUALITIE)
DECEIT	My Lord, we have with diligence Bucklit up weel yon bletheran' bard!
SPIRITUALITIE	I think you deserve gude recompence. Tak thir ten crowns for your reward!
	(CHASTITIE *enters*)
CHASTITIE	(*Song*) *Quantus tremor est futurus,* *Quando iudex est venturus,* *Cuncta stricte discurssuns[1].*
	(*The* THREE VICES *move out of the picture a little*)
	How lang sal this inconstant warld endure That I should banished be sae lang, alas! Few crëatures, or nane, taks of me cure, Whilk gars me mony a nicht lie harbourless!
DILIGENCE	Lady, I pray you show to me your name!
CHASTITIE	Dame Chastitie, banished without a hame!
DILIGENCE	Then pass to ladies of Religion, Whilk maks their vows to observe Chastity. Lo, where there sits ane Prioress of renoun Amang the rest of Spiritualitie!
	(DILIGENCE *points out the* PRIORESS, *who is one of the members of the* SPIRITUAL ESTAIT)
CHASTITIE	(*to* DILIGENCE) I grant yon Lady has vowit chastity, For her profession thereto should accord. She made that vow for ane abbacy, But nocht for Christ Jesus our Lord . . . I sall observe your counsel if I may; Come on, and hear what yon lady will say.
	(CHASTITIE *and* DILIGENCE *approach the* PRIORESS)

[1] what trembling there will be when the
judge is come and dashes everything to
pieces.

<table>
<tr><td></td><td>(to PRIORESS)
My prudent, lusty Lady Prioress,
Remember how ye did vow chastity;
Madame, I pray you of your gentleness
That ye wad please to have of me pity
And this ae nicht to give me harboury!</td></tr>
<tr><td>PRIORESS</td><td>Pass hence, Madame, by Christ ye come not here!
Ye are contrair to my complexion!
Gang seek lodging at some auld monk or friar,
Perchance they will be your protection.
Or to prelates mak your progression
Whilk are obliged to you as weel as I!
Dame Sensual has given direction
You to exclude out of my company!</td></tr>
<tr><td></td><td>(CHASTITIE now
addresses the LORDS OF
SPIRITUALITIE)</td></tr>
<tr><td>CHASTITIE</td><td>Lords, I have passed throw mony uncouth shire,
But in this land I can get nae lodging!
Of my name if ye wad have knowledging
Forsooth, my lords, they call me Chastitie.
I you beseek of your graces benign,
Give me lodging this nicht for charity!</td></tr>
<tr><td>SPIRITUALITIE</td><td>Pass on, Madame, we know you nocht!
Or by Him that the warld has wrocht,
Your coming sall be richt dear bocht,
       If ye mak langer tarry!</td></tr>
<tr><td>ABBOT</td><td>But doubt we will baith live and die
       With our love Sensualitie:
We will have nae mair deal with thee
       Than with the Queen of Fairy.</td></tr>
<tr><td>PARSON</td><td>Pass hame amang the Nuns and dwell
       Whilk are of chastity the well —
I trust they will with book and bell
       Receive you in their cloister!</td></tr>
<tr><td>CHASTITIE</td><td>Sir, when I was the Nuns amang,
Out of their dorter they me dang.[1]
And wad not let me bide sae lang
       As say my Paternoster.
I see nae grace there for to get.
I hauld it best, or it be late,
For to go prove the temporal state
       Gif they will me receive.</td></tr>
</table>

[1] beat

(CHASTITIE crosses to the
TEMPORAL ESTAIT)

CHASTITIE   Gude-day, my Lord Temporalitie,
(Contd)   And you, Merchant of gravity;
                 Full fain wad I have harboury,
                         To lodge amang the lave.[1]

TEMPORALITIE   Forsooth we wad be weel content
                 To harbour you with gude intent,
                 Were it not we have impediment —
                         For why? We twa are marryit!

MERCHANT   And wist our wives that ye were here,
                 They wad mak all this toun on steer,[2]
                 Therefore we rede you, rin arear,
                 In dreid ye be miscarryit!

(CHASTITIE now goes to the
Common People, who receive
her)

CHASTITIE   Ye men of craft and great ingyne,[3]
                 Give me harboury for Christës pyne.

(SOUTAR[4] and TAILOR are
both a little too civil)

SOUTAR   Is this fair Lady Chastitie?

TAILOR   Now welcome by the Trinity!

SOUTAR   Sit doun, Madame, and tak a drink,
                 And let nae sorrow in you sink!

(They receive CHASTITIE)

SOUTAR'S WIFE   What does the Soutar, my guid-man?

TAILOR'S WIFE   Marry, fills the cup and tooms[5] the can
                 Wi a fair maiden clad in white,
                 In whom the lurdan taks delight —
                 I trust, if I can reckon richt,
                 She shapes to lodge wi him all nicht!
                 Ere he come hame, by God I trow,
                 He will be drunken like a sow!

SOUTAR'S WIFE   This is a great despite, I think,
                 For to receive sic ane cow-clink![6]
                 What is your counsel that we do?

TAILOR'S WIFE   Cummer, this is my counsel, lo!
                 Ding ye the tane, and I the tother!

SOUTAR'S WIFE   I am content, by Goddës Mother!
                 I think for me, thae hure-son smaiks

---

[1]rest [2]uproar [3]ability [4]Shoemaker [5]empties [5]prostitute

	Deserve richt weel to get their paiks!
	What, Master Fiend, needs all this haste?
	For it is half ane year almaist
	Sen ever that loon laboured my leather!
TAILOR'S WIFE	God let my tricker grace a tether!
	For it is mair than forty days
	Sen ever he cleikit up my claes!
	If they have given us sic despite
	Let us gae ding them till they dryte.[1]

(*But first they drive* CHASTITIE
away)

Go hence, harlot, how durst thou be sae bauld
To lodge with our gudemen without licence?
I mak a vow by Him that Judas sauld,
This rock of mine sall be thy recompence!

SOUTAR'S WIFE	Show me thy name, duddron,[2] with diligence!
CHASTITIE	Marry, Chastitie is my name, by Saint Blaise.
SOUTAR'S WIFE	I pray God may he work on thee vengeance
	For I lovit ne'er Chastitie all my days!

(*She pursues* CHASTITIE *with
her spinning rock. The* WIVES
turn on their husbands)

I mak ane vow to St. Crispin,
I'se be revengit on that graceless groom!
And to begin the play, tak there ane flap!

(*She strikes the* SOUTAR)

SOUTAR	The fiend receive the hands that gave me that!
SOUTAR'S WIFE	What now, hure-son, begins thou for till ban?
	Tak there another upon thy peeled harn-pan![3]
	(*to* TAILOR'S WIFE)
	What now, cummer, will thou nocht tak my part?
TAILOR'S WIFE	That sall I do, cummer, with all my heart.

(*The* WIVES *chase* SOUTAR *and*
TAILOR *round the stage and back
to their places, where they sit, both
sadder and wiser.* CHASTITIE *has
returned to the protection of*
DILIGENCE.
SOLACE *now catches sight of*
CHASTITIE *and speaks to the*
KING)

---

[1]defecate [2]slut [3]bald cranium

SOLACE	Sovereign, get up and see ane heavenly sicht,
	Ane fair lady in white aboulyament![1]
	She may be peer unto a king or Knight,
	Maist like an angel by my judgëment!

(The KING rises from among the LADIES)

KING	I sall gang see that sicht incontinent.
	(to SENSUALITIE)
	Madame, behauld if ye have knawledging
	Of yon lady, or what is her intent.
	Thereafter we sall turn but tarrying.

SENSUALITIE	Sir, let me see what yon matter may mean —
	Perchance that I may know her by her face.

(She looks more closely at CHASTITIE)

	But doubt, this is Dame Chastitie, I ween!
	Sir, I and she cannot bide in ane place!
	But if it be the pleasure of your grace,
	That I remain into your company,
	This woman richt hastily gar chase,
	That she nae mair be seen in this country!

KING	As ever ye please, sweetheart, sae sall it be!
	Dispone her as ye think expedient.
	Even as ye list to let her live or die,
	I will refer that thing to your judgement.

(The KING reclines again while SENSUALITIE gives orders)

SENSUALITIE	I will that she be banished incontinent,
	And never to come again in this country;
	And if she does, but doubt she sall repent,
	Also perchance a duleful deid sall die!
	Pass on, Sir Sapience and Discretion,
	And banish her out of the King's presence!

DECEIT	That sall we do, Madame, by God's passion!
	We sall do thy command with diligence
	And at your hand deserve good recompence.
	Dame Chastitie, come on, be not aghast!
	We sall richt soon upon your ain expense
	Into the stocks your bonny foot mak fast!

(The THREE VICES fasten CHASTITIE to the stocks)

[1]clothing

CHASTITIE	(*to* VERITIE) Sister, alas, this is a care-full case, That we with princes should be sae abhorred!
VERITIE	Be blithe, sister, I trust within short space That we sall be richt honourably restored, And with the King we sall be at concord, For I hear tell Divine Correction Is new landit, thankit be Christ our Lord! I wat he will be our protection.
	(*A fanfare. Enter* CORRECTION'S VARLET)

VARLET	Sirs, stand aback and hauld you coy.
	I am the King Correction's boy,
	      Come here to dress his place!
	See that you mak obedience
	Unto his noble excellence,
	      Fra time you see his face!
	For he maks reformations
	Out-throw all Christian nations,
	      Where he finds great debates.
	And sae far as I understand,
	He sall reform into this land,
	      Even all the Thrie Estaites.
	For silence I protest
	Baith of Lord, Laird and Lady!
	Now will I rin but rest,
	      And tell that all is ready!

	(*Fanfare. Exit* CORRECTION'S VARLET. *The* THREE VICES *go into a huddle*)

DECEIT	Brother, hear ye yon proclamation?
	I dreid full sair of reformation,
	      Yon message maks me mangit![1]
	What is your counsel, to me tell!
	Remain we here, by God himsel,
	      We will be all three hangit!

FLATTERIE	I'll gang to Spiritualitie,
	And preach out-throw his diosee,
	      Where I will be unknawn,
	Or keep me close into some cloister
	With mony a piteous Paternoster,
	      Till all their blasts be blawn.

DECEIT	I'll be weel treatit, as ye ken, With my maisters the merchant men,

[1] confounded

DECEIT (Contd)	Whilk can mak small debate; Ye ken richt few of them that thrives Or can beguile the landwart[1] wives Without their man, Deceit. Now, Falsehood, what sall be thy shift?
FALSEHOOD	Na, care thou not, man, for my thrift! Trows thou that I be daft? Na, I will live a lusty life Withouten ony sturt or strife Amang the men of craft!
DECEIT	Falsehood, I wad we made a bond Now, while the King is yet sleepand, What rack to steal his box?
FALSEHOOD	Now, weel said, by the Sacrament. I sall it steal incontinent, Though it had twenty locks!

(FALSEHOOD *steals the* KING'S
box)

	Lo, here the Box! Now let us gae. This may suffice for our rewards.
DECEIT	Yea, that it may, man, by this day! It may weel mak us landwart lairds! Now let us cast away our claes, In dreid some follow on the chase!
FALSEHOOD	Richt weel devisit, man, by Saint Blaise, Wad God we were out of this place!

(*Here they take off their
counterfeit clothes*)

DECEIT	Now, sen there is nae man to wrang us, I pray you, brother, with my heart, Let us gae part this pelf amang us, Syne hastily we sall depart!
FALSEHOOD	Trows thou to get as meikle as I? That sall thou nocht! I stole the box! Thou did naething but lookit by, Aye lurkan' like a wily fox!

(DECEIT *and* FALSEHOOD
fight)

	Alas for ever my eye is out!
DECEIT	Upon thy craig[2] tak there a clout!

[1]country [2]neck

(In the meantime FLATTERIE
*takes the box and runs out
pursued by* FALSEHOOD *and*
DECEIT. *Their flight is
hastened by a fanfare and stately
march. Enter* DIVINE
CORRECTION *with his retinue)*

CORRECTION | I am callit Divine Correction
Where I am nocht, is nae tranquillity!
By me traitors and tyrants are put doun,
Wha thinks nae shame of their iniquity!
I am ane judge, richt potent and severe,
Come to dae justice mony a thousand mile.
I am sae constant, baith in peace and weir,
Nae bribe nor favour may my sicht ower-sile.[1]
What is ane King? Nocht but ane officer,
To cause his lieges live in equity,
And under God to be a punisher,
Of trespassers against His Majesty.

GUDE COUNSEL | Welcome, my lord, welcome ten thousand times
To all the true men of this region!
Welcome for to correct all faults and crimes
Amang this cankered congregation!
Lowse Chastity, I mak supplication,
Put to freedom fair Lady Verity,
Wha, by unfaithful folk of this nation,
Lies bound full fast into captivity!

CORRECTION | I marvel, Gude Counsel, how that may be —
Are ye nocht with the King familiar?

GUDE COUNSEL | That I am nocht, my lord, full wae is me
But like a beggar am haulden at the bar!

CORRECTION | Where lies yon ladies in captivity?

(Turning to VERITIE *and*
CHASTITIE *in stocks)*

How now, sisters, wha has you so disguisit?

VERITIE | Unfaithful members of inquity,
Despitefully, my Lord, has us suppressed.

CORRECTION | Had I them here, thae knaves should ken my knocks,
That them oppressed and banished from this land!
Gang, put yon ladies to their liberty
Incontinent, and break doun all stocks!
But doubt, they are full dear welcome to me!
Mak diligence, methinks ye do but mocks!

[1] obscure

CORRECTION (Contd)	Speed, men, and spare not for to break the locks, And tenderly to tak them by the hand!

*(VERITIE and CHASTITIE
are released. The COURTIERS spy
CORRECTION)*

WANTONNESS	Solace, knaws thou not what I see? Ane knicht, or else ane king thinks me, Brother, what may this mean?
SOLACE	Whether that he be friend or fae, Stand still, and hear what he will say, Sic ane I have not seen!
PLACEBO	I rede us, put upon the King, And wauken him out of his sleeping!

(He rouses the KING)

Sir, rise and see an unco thing!
           Get up, ye lie too lang!

*(The KING has been in the
arms of SENSUALITIE, who
resents the interference
and rates PLACEBO)*

SENSUALITIE	Put on your hood, John-fool! Ye rave! How dare ye be sae pert, Sir Knave, To touch the King? Sae Christ me save, False hure-son, thou sall hang!

*(CORRECTION approaches the
KING)*

CORRECTION	Get up, Sir King, ye have sleepit eneuch Intil the arms of Lady Sensual!

*(The KING rises and faces
CORRECTION)*

Remember how, into the time of Noy[1]
For the foul stink and sin of lechery,
God by my wand did all the warld destroy.
Sodom and Gomorra richt sae full rigorously
For that vile sin were brunt[2] maist cruelly.
Therefore I thee command, incontinent
Banish from thee that hure Sensualitie
Or beyond doubt rudely thou sall repent!

KING	By whom have ye sae great authority? Wha does presume for to correct a King? Know ye not me, great King Humanitie, That in my region royally does reign?

[1]Noah [2]burned

CORRECTION	I have power great princes to doun-thring,
	That lives contrair the Majesty Divine,
	Against the truth whilk plainly does malign;
	Repent they not, I put them to ruine!
	I will begin at thee, whilk is the head,
	And mak on thee first reformation,
	Thy lieges then will follow thee indeed!
	Swith, harlot, hence without dilation![1]

(The last line is addressed
to SENSUALITIE)

SENSUALITIE	My Lord, I mak you supplication,
	Give me licence to pass again to Rome!
CORRECTION	Amang the princes of that nation.
	I let you wit[2] your fresh beauty will bloom!
SENSUALITIE	Adieu, Sir King, I mae nae langer tarry!
	Not that I care, as gude love comes as gaes!
	I recommend you to the Queen of Fairy —
	I see ye will be guided by my faes!

(SENSUALITIE, *with* HAMELI-
NESS *and* DANGER, *passes to the*
SPIRITUAL ESTAIT)

My lordes of the Spiritual State,
Venus preserve you air[3] and late!
For I can mak nae mair debate,
       I am partit with your king,
And am banished this region,
By counsel of Correction.
Be ye not my protection,
       I may seek my lodging!

SPIRITUALITIE	Welcome, our days' darling!
	Welcome with all our heart!
	We without feigning
	Sall plainly tak your part!

(*The* BISHOPS, ABBOTS
and PARSONS *kiss the ladies.*
SENSUALITIE, HAMELINESS,
DANGER *take their places with*
SPIRITUAL ESTAIT.
SENSUALITIE *pairing with*
SPIRITUALITIE, HAMELINESS
with ABBOT *and* DANGER *with*
PARSON)

[1]delay   [2]I am sure   [3]early

CORRECTION	Sen you are quit of Sensualitie,
	Receive into your service Gude Counsel.
	And richt so this fair Lady Chastitie,
	Till ye marry some queen of blude-royal.
	Observe then Chastity matrimonial.
	Richt so receive Veritie by the hand . . .
	Use their counsel, your fame sall never fall;
	With them therefore mak ane perpetual band!
	Now sir tak tent to what I say
	Observe thir same baith nicht and day
	And let them never part you frae,
	Or else withouten doubt,
	Turn ye to Sensuality,
	To vicious life and ribaldry,
	Out of your realm richt shamefully
	Ye sall be rootit out.
KING	I am content to your counsel t'incline.
	At your command sall be all that is mine!
	(*The* KING *embraces*
	CORRECTION *humbly. There fol-*
	lows
	a ceremony of purification)
CORRECTION	Now steek your cries of "Waylaway!"
	Enough, contrition has its day,
	The hour demands remeid!
	Tis not eneuch to beat the breist
	And weep saut tears, I tell you neist
	Repent by active deed!
	I counsel you incontinent,
	To gar proclaim ane Parliament
	Of all the Thrie Estaites,
	That they be here with diligence
	To mak to you obedience,
	And syne dress all debates!
KING	That sall be done, but mair demand.
	Ho, Diligence, come here frae hand[1]
	And tak your information.
	Gang, warn the Spiritualitie,
	Richt sae the Temporalitie,
	By open proclamation,
	In gudlie haste for to compear[2]
	In their maist honourable maneer[3]
	To give us their counsels!
	Wha that beis absent, to them shaw
	That they sall under-lie the law

[1]at once [2]assemble [3]manner

	And punished be that fails!
DILIGENCE	Sir, I sall baith in burgh and land,
	With diligence do your command,
	Upon my ain expense.
	Sir, I have servit you all this year,
	But I gat never ane dinner
	Yet for my recompence!
KING	Pass on, and thou sall be regardit
	And for thy service weel rewardit,
	For why, with my consent,
	Thou sall have yearly for thy hire
	The teind mussels of the Ferry-Mire
	Confirmit in Parliament.
DILIGENCE	(*sourly to the audience*)
	I will get riches throw that rent
	After the day of Doom,
	When in the coal-pits of Tranent
	Butter will grow on broom!
	All nicht I had sae meikle drouth,
	I micht not sleep ane wink,
	Or I proclaim ocht with my mouth,
	But doubt I maun have drink!

(DILIGENCE *goes to refresh
himself in sight of the
audience as a preparation
for the proclamation he
will shortly make.
Now* CORRECTION *tackles the*
COURTIERS)

CORRECTION	Come here, Placebo and Solace,
	With your companion Wantonness,
	I know weel your condition.
	For enticing King Humanitie
	To receive Sensualitie
	You maun suffer punition!
WANTONNESS	We grant, my Lord, we have done ill;
	Therefore we put us in your will,
	But we have been abusit!
PLACEBO	For in gude faith, sir, we believit
	That lechery had nae man grievit,
	Because it was sae usit!
SOLACE	Sir, we sall mend our condition
	Sae ye give us remission . . .

SOLACE (Contd)	But give us leave to sing, To dance, to play at chess and tables, To read stories and merry fables For pleasure of our King.
CORRECTION	For why as I suppose, Princes may some time seek solace With mirth and lawful merriness, Their spirits to rejoice. And richt sae Hawking and Hunting Are honest pastimes for ane King, Into the time of peace; And learn to rin ane heavy spear, That he into the time of weir May follow at the chase. See that ye dae nae other crime. Ye sall be pardonit at this time.
KING	Where is Sapience and Discretion? And why comes not Devotion near?
VERITIE	They three were Flatterie and Deceit And Falsehood, that unhappy loon. Against us three whilk made debate, And banished us from toun to toun.
CHASTITIE	They gart us twa fall in a swoon, When they us lockit in the stocks. That dastard knave, Discretion, Full thefteously did steal your box!
KING	The devil tak them, sen they are gane! I mak a vow to sweet Saint Fillan, When I them find, they'll bear their paiks,[1] I see they have playit me the glaiks![2] Gude Counsel, now show me the best, How I sall keep my realm in rest.
GUDE COUNSEL	The principal point, sir, of ane king's office, Is for to do to every man justice, And for to mix his justice with mercy, Without rigour, favour or partiality, Wha guides them weel, they win immortal fame; Wha the contrair, they get perpetual shame. The Chronicles to know, I you exhort; There sall ye find baith gude and evil report; For every prince, after his quality, Though he be deid, his deeds sall never die! Sir, if you please for to use my counsel, Your fame and name sall be perpetual.

[1]punishment [2]deception

	(DILIGENCE *has finished his*
	drink. A fanfare)
DILIGENCE	Hoyez, hoyez, hoyez!
	At the command of King Humanitie
	I warn and charge all members of Parliament,
	Baith Spiritual State and Temporalitie,
	That to his grace they be obedient,
	And speed them to the court, incontinent,
	I gude order, arrayit royally.
	Wha beis absent or inobedient
	The King's pleasure they sall under-lie!
	(*to the audience*)
	Also I mak you exhortation,
	Since ye have heard the first part of our play,
	Go, tak ane drink and mak collation;
	Ilk man drink to his marrow, I you pray.
	Tarry nocht lang, it is late in the day.
	Let some drink ale, and some drink claret wine;
	By great Doctors of Physic I hear say
	That michty drink comforts them dull ingyne![1]

(*Music. A march. All go off.*)

THE END OF THE FIRST PART OF THE SATYRE

.

[1]intellect

Danger, Dame Sensualitie and Hameliness

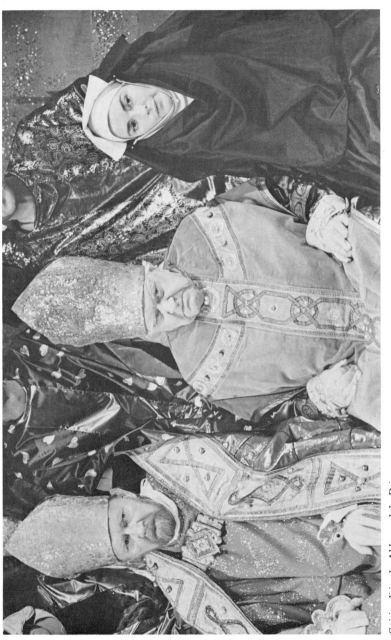

Spiritualitie, the Abbot and the Prioress

Falsehood, King Humanitie, Deceit and Flatterie

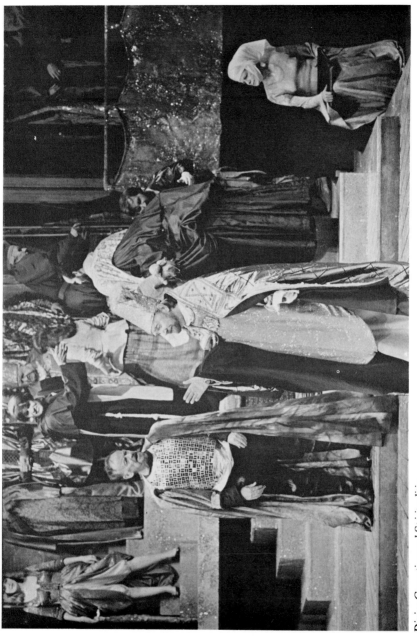

Divine Correction and Spiritualite

Diligence

Dame Sensualitie

Gude Counsel.

King Humanitie

John the Common-Weal

THE SECOND PART

(Music. DILIGENCE comes on to the empty stage as if to make an announcement)

DILIGENCE   Famous people, tak tent . . . .

(The POOR MAN hurries on, appealing for alms)

POOR MAN   Of your alms, gude folk, for God's love of heaven
For I have motherless bairns either sax or seven!
If ye'll give me nae gude, for the love of Jesus,
Show me the richt way to Saint Andrews.

DILIGENCE   Where have we gotten this gudely companion?
Swith! Furth of the field, thou false, ragged loon!
Officers, come chase this carle away,
Or deil a word ye'se get mair of our play!

(The POOR MAN climbs up on the KING'S throne)

Come doun, or by God's croun, false loon I sall slay thee!

POOR MAN   Now swear by thy brunt shins, the devill ding them frae ye!

DILIGENCE   Swith, beggar bogle, haste thee away,
Thou art over pert to spoil our play!

POOR MAN   I will give for your play not a sow's fart
For there is richt little play at my hungry heart!

DILIGENCE   What devill ails this cruikit carle?

POOR MAN   Marry, meikle sorrow.
I cannot get, though I gasp, to beg nor to borrow.

DILIGENCE   Where dwells thou, bankrupt, or what is thine intent?

POOR MAN   I dwell into Lothian ane mile fra Tranent.

DILIGENCE   Where wad thou be, carle? The sooth to me show!

POOR MAN   Sir, even to St. Andrews for to seek law.

DILIGENCE   For to seek law, in Edinburgh is the nearest way.

POOR MAN   Sir, I socht law there this mony a dear day;
But I could get nane at Session or Senate,
Therefore the meikle dumb devill droun all that menyie![1]

DILIGENCE   Show me thy matter, man, with all the circumstance,
How thou has happenit on this unhappy chance.

POOR MAN   Gude man, will ye give me of your charitie
And I sall declare you the black veritie:
How halie kirk by mony a toll and tax

[1]pack

POOR MAN (Contd)	Laid to my life its merciless greedy axe. My faither was an auld man and a hair[1] And was of age fourscore of years and mair, And Maud my mother was fourscore and fifteen; And with my labour I did them both sustain. We had a Mare that carrit salt and coal, And every year she brocht us hame a foal. We had three kye that was baith fat and fair, Nane tidier hence to the toun of Ayr. My faither was sae weak of blude and bane, That he deit, wherefore my mother made great mane,[2] Then she deit within ane day or twa, And there began my poverty and woe. Our guid grey mare was grazan' on the field And our land's laird took her for his hire-yield.[3] Then, like the hoodie craws, when owre the rocks A lamb has fa'en, they cam in hungry flocks. Our vicar took the best cow by the heid Incontinent, when my faither was deid. And when the vicar heard tell how that my mother Was deid, frae hand he took frae me another. Then Meg my wife did mourn baith even and morrow Till at the last she deit for very sorrow. And when the vicar heard tell my wife was deid, The third cow he cleikit[4] by the heid. Their hinmost claes that was of rapploch grey,[5] The vicar gart his clerk bear them away. When all was gane I micht mak nae debate, But with my bairns passed for to beg my meat. Now have I told you the black veritie How I am brocht into this misery.
DILIGENCE	How did the Parson? Was he not thy gude friend?
POOR MAN	The devil stick him, he curst me for my teind[6] And haulds me yet under that same process That gart me want the Sacrament at Pace.[7] In gude faith, sir, though ye wad cut my throat, I have nae gear except ane English groat Whilk I purpose to give ane man of law.
DILIGENCE	Thou art the daftest fule that ever I saw! Trow thou, man, by the law, to get remeid Of men of Kirk? Na, never till thou be deid! Be sure of priests thou will get nae support.
POOR MAN	Gif that be true, the fiend receive the sort! Sae, sen I see I get nae other grace,

---

[1]with white hair [2]mean [3]fine [4]caught [5]coarse cloth [6]tithe [7]Easter

I will lie doun and rest me in this place.

*(He does so. Opening music is
repeated)*

DILIGENCE   Famous people . . . tak tent . . .

(Enter PARDONER*)*

PARDONER   Bona dies, bona dies!
Devout people, gude day I say you
Now tarry a little while I pray you
        Till I be with you known!
Wat ye weel how I am namit?
Ane noble man and undefamit,
        If all the sooth were shown.
I am Sir Robert Rome-raker,
A perfyte public pardoner
        Admittit by the Pape.
Sirs, I sall show you, for my wage,
My pardons and my pilgrimage,
        Whilk ye sall see and graip.[1]
I give to the devil with gude intent
This woeful wicked New Testament,
        With them that it translatit.
Sen laymen knew the verity,
Pardoners gets nae charity
        Without that they debate it.
Deil fell the brain that has it wroucht,
Sae fall them that the Buik hame brocht,
        Also I pray to the Rood
That Martin Luther, that false loon,
Black Bullenger and Melancthoun
        Had been smored in their cude.[2]
By Him that bure the croun of thorn
I wad Saint Paul had never been born.
        Also I wad his buiks
Were never read into the Kirk
But amang friars into the mirk
        Or riven amang the rocks!

(He exhibits his wares)

My patent pardons ye may see
Come frae the Khan of Tartary
        Weel sealed with oyster shells.
Though ye have nae contrition
Ye sall have full remission
        With help of books and bells.
Here is ane relic, lang and braid,

---

[1]grasp [2]smothered in their christening gown

PARDONER
(Contd)
	Of Finn MacColl the richt chaft blade[1]
	    With teeth and all together.
	Of Colin's cow here is a horn
	For eating of MacConnel's corn
	    Was slain into Balquhidder.
	Here is ane cord baith great and lang,
	Whilk hangit Johnnie the Armstrang,
	    Of gude hemp soft and sound.
	Gude haly people, I stand for'd,
	Wha ever beis hangit with this cord
	    Needs never be dround!
	Come win the pardon, now let see,
	For meal, for malt or for money,
	    For cock, hen, goose or grice![2]
	Of relics here I have ane hunder.
	Why come ye nocht? This is ane wonder.
	    I trow ye be not wise!
	
	(*The* PARDONER'S BOY,
	WILKIN, *enters calling*)

WILKIN	Ho, maister, ho, where are ye now?
PARDONER	I am here, Wilkin Widdifow.
WILKIN	Sir, I have done your bidding, For I have found a great horse-bane, A fairer saw ye never nane, Upon Tom Flesher's midden. Sir, ye may gar the wifeis trow It is a bane of Saint Bride's cow! Gif, sir, ye rule this relic weill All haill the wives will kiss and kneel, Betwixt this and Dumbartane.
PARDONER	Thou has done weill by God's mother! Tak ye the tane and I the tother, Sae sall we mak great cheer . . . (*He takes the horse-bone and* WILKIN *the horn which he blows loudly. The* POOR MAN *wakes up*)
POOR MAN	What thing was yon that I heard crack and cry? I have been dreaman' and drivellan' of my kye! With my richt hand my hail body I sain[3] Saint Bride, Saint Bride, send me my kye again!
PARDONER	Bona Dies, Bona Dies.
POOR MAN	(*Spying* PARDONER)

[1] jaw bone   [2] pig   [3] bless

I see standan' yonder a haly man;
To mak me help, let me see if he can! Haly maister!

PARDONER Come win the pardon, and syne I sall thee sain!

POOR MAN Will that pardon get my kye again?

PARDONER Carle, of thy kye I have nothing ado.
Come win my pardon, and kiss my relics too!

(He sains him with his relics)

Now lowse thy purse, and lay doun thy offrand,
And thou sall have my pardon even frae-hand.
Now win the pardon, limmer,[1] or thou art lost!

POOR MAN My haly faither, what will that pardon cost?

PARDONER Let see what siller thou bearest in thy bag.

POOR MAN I have ane groat here bound into a rag.

PARDONER Has thou no other siller but ane groat?

POOR MAN If I have mair, sir, come and rip my coat!

PARDONER Give me that groat, man, if thou hasts nae mair.

POOR MAN With all my heart, maister, lo, tak it, there!
Now let me see your pardon, with your leave.

PARDONER Ane thousand year of pardons I thee give!

POOR MAN Ane thousand year? I will not live sae lang.
Deliver me it, maister, and let me gang.

PARDONER Ane thousand year I lay upon thy heid,
With *totiens quotiens*[2]; now mak nae mair plead.
Thou hast receivit thy pardon now already.

POOR MAN But I can see naething, sir, by our Lady!

PARDONER What craves the carle? Me thinks thou art not wise!

POOR MAN I crave my groat, or else my merchandise.

PARDONER I gave thee pardon for a thousand year!

POOR MAN How sall I get that pardon? Let me hear!

PARDONER Stand still, and I sall tell thee the haill story!
When thou art deid and gaes to Purgatory,
Being condemned to pain a thousand year,
Then sall thy pardon thee relieve but weir![3]
Now be content! Ye are ane marvellous man!

POOR MAN Sall I get nothing for my groat till then?

PARDONER That sall thou not! I mak it to you plain!

(POOR MAN is now very angry)

POOR MAN Na? Then, gossip, give me my groat again!

---

[1]rascal   [2]with multiples; if necessary   [3]without doubt

POOR MAN (Contd)	What say ye, maisters? Call ye this gude reason, That he should promise me a gude pardon, And here receive my money in this stead, Syne mak me nae payment till I be deid? When I am deid, I wat, full sickerly, My silly saul will pass to Purgatory. Declare me this! Now God nor Belial bind thee, When I am there, curst carle, where sall I find thee? Not into heaven, but rather into hell! When thou art there, thou cannot help thysel!
PARDONER	Swith, stand aback! I trow this man be mangit! Thou gets not this groat, though thou should be hangit!
POOR MAN	Give me my groat, weel bound into my clout! Or, by God's breid, Robin sall bear a rout! *(He sets upon the* PARDONER, *and chases him off. He casts the relics away)*
DILIGENCE	What kind of daffing is this all day? Swift, smaiks[1] out of the field, away! Into a prison put them soon Syne hang them when the play is done! *(A fanfare and march which continue through ensuing speeches)* *(Enter* KING, CORRECTION, COURTIERS, VIRTUES. *They take their places)*
DILIGENCE	Famous people, tak tent, and ye sall see The Thrie Estaites of this nation, Come to the Court with ane strange gravity. Therefore I mak you supplication Till ye have heard our haill narration To keep silence and be patient I pray you. Howbeit we speak by adulation We sall say nothing but the sooth, I say you!
WANTONNESS	Now braid *benedicite!* What thing is yon that I see? Look, Solace, my heart!
SOLACE	Brother Wantonness, what thinks thou? Yon are the Thrie Estaites, I trow, Gangand backwart!

[1]rascals

WANTONNESS	Backwart? Backwart? Out! Waylaway!
	It is great shame for them, I say,
	          Backwart to gang.
	I trow the King Correction
	Maun mak a reformation,
	          Or it be lang!
	Now let us go and tell the King!

(The COURTIERS *approach
the* KING*)*

Sir, we have seen ane marvellous thing,
          By our judgement!
The Thrie Estaites of this Region,
Are comand backwart, throw this toun,
          To the Parliament!

KING	Backwart, backwart, how may that be? Gar speed them hastily to me, In dreid that they gae wrang!
PLACEBO	Sir, I see them yonder command, They will be here even frae hand, As fast as they may gang!

GUDE COUNSEL	Sir, hald you still and scare them nocht,
	Till ye perceive what be their thocht,
	          And see what men them leads.
	And let the King Correction
	Mak ane sharp inquisition,
	          And mark them by the heids!

(The THRIE ESTAITES
enter, singing, led by the
VICES. *They are
"gangand backward",
each led by their vices).*

SPIRITUALITIE	*(singing)* Gloire, honour, laud, triumph and victory, Here are we come, all the Estaites Thrie, Ready to mak our due obedience, At your command with humble observance.
TEMPORALITIE	*(singing)* Sir, we, with michty courage at command Of your super-excellent Majesty, Sall mak service baith with our heart and hand, We are content, that we may see That noble, heavenly King Correction.

CORRECTION	My tender friends, I pray you with my heart,
	Declare to me the thing that I wad speir.
	What is the cause that ye gang all backwart?
	The verity thereof fain wad I hear.
SPIRITUALITIE	Sovereign, we have gone sae this mony a year.
	Howbeit ye think we go undecently,
	We think we gang richt wonder pleasantly.
DILIGENCE	Sit doun, my lords, into your proper places:
	Syne let the King consider all sic cases.
	Sit doun, Sir Scribe, Provost and Baillies too
	And fence¹ the Court as ye were wont to do.

(*The* ESTAITES *sit and*
GUDE COUNSEL *passes to*
his seat)

KING	My prudent lordës of the Thrie Estaites,
	It is our will, above all other thing,
	For to reform all them that maks debates
	Contrair the richt, whilk daily does malign,
	And they that does the Common-Weal doun-thring.
	With help and counsel of King Correction,
	It is our will for to mak punishing,
	And plain oppressors put to subjection.
SPIRITUALITIE	What thing is this, sir, that ye have devisit?
	Sirs, ye have need for to be weel advisit.
	Be not hasty into your execution,
	And be not owre extreme in your punition.
	And if ye please to do, sir, as we say,
	Postpone this Parliament till ane other day.
	For why? The people of this region
	May not endure extreme correction!
CORRECTION	My Lords, is this the part that ye will tak
	To mak us supportation to correct?
	It does appear that ye are culpable,
	That are not to Correction appliable!
	Swift, Diligence, gae show it is our will,
	That every man oppressed give in his bill.

(*A trumpet sounds*)

DILIGENCE	All manner of men I warn that be oppressed
	Come and complain and they sall be redressed.
	It is the noble Prince's will
	That ilk complainer sall give in his bill.
JOHN	Out of my gait! For God's sake let me gae!
	Tell me again, gude maister, what ye say.

¹proclaim

	(JOHN *the* COMMON-WEAL *emerges from the audience*)
DILIGENCE	I warn all that be wrangously offendit Come and complain and they sall be amendit. What is thy name, fellow? That I would feel.
JOHN	Forsooth they call me John the Common-Weal.
DILIGENCE	Come over, and I sall show thee to his grace.
	(DILIGENCE *leads* JOHN *before* KING *and* CORRECTION)
JOHN	God's benison licht in that lucky face!
KING	Show me thy name, gude man, I thee command.
JOHN	Marry, John the Common-Weal of fair Scotland.
	(*The* KING *surveys* JOHN'S *rags*)
KING	The Common-Weal has been amang his faes.
JOHN	Yea, sir. That gars the Common-Weal want claes!
KING	What is the cause the Common-Weal is cruikit?
JOHN	Because the Common-Weal has been owrelookit.
KING	What gars thee look sae with ane dreary heart?
JOHN	Because the Thrie Estaites gangs all backwart.
KING	Sir Common-Weal, know ye the limmers that them leads?
JOHN	Their canker colours I ken them by the heids! As for our reverend fathers of Spiritualitie, They are led by Flatterie and careless Sensualitie, And as ye see, Temporalitie has need of correction, Whilk has lang time been led by Public Oppression. Lo, here is Falsehood, and Deceit weel I ken, Leaders of the merchants and silly crafts-men. What marvel though the Thrie Estaites backwart gang, When sic ane vile company dwells them amang, Whilk has rulit this rout mony dear days, Whilk gars John the Common-Weal want his warm claes. Thou feignit Flatterie, the fiend fart in thy face! When ye was guider of the court we gat little grace! My sovereign Lord Correction I mak you supplication, Put these tryed trickers from Christ's congregation!
CORRECTION	As ye have devisit, but doubt it sall be done! Come here, my Sergeants, and do your debt soon! Put thir three pillours into prison strang Howbeit ye should hang them, ye do them nae wrang!

FIRST SERGEANT	Sovereign Lord, we sall obey your commands. Brother, upon thae limmers lay on your hands!
SECOND SERGEANT	Come here, gossip, come here, come here! Your reckless life ye sall repent! When was ye wont to be sae sweir?[1] Stand still and be obedient!

(On these speeches the SERGEANTS hustle DECEIT and FALSEHOOD and put them unwillingly in the stocks)

SECOND SERGEANT	Put in your legs into the stocks, For ye had never meeter hose! Thir stewats stinks as they were brocks![2] Now are ye siccar,[3] I suppose!

(The SERGEANTS go to CORRECTION)

FIRST SERGEANT	My Lord, we have done your commands, Sall we put Flatterie in captivity?
CORRECTION	Yea, hardly lay on him your hands! Richt sae upon Sensualitie.

(SERGEANTS put FLATTERIE in stocks. SENSUALITIE turns to SPIRITUALITIE)

SENSUALITIE	Adieu, my lord!
SPIRITUALITIE	Adieu, my ain sweet heart! Now dule fall me that we twa maun part!
SENSUALITIE	My lord, howbeit this parting does me pain, I traist in God we sall meet soon again!
SPIRITUAL ESTAIT	Adieu! Adieu! Adieu!
SENSUALITIE	*(sings)* Adieu! Lovers beware and tak gude heed Whom that ye love, for whom ye suffer pain. Unconstant is desire. Therefore I rede: Seek ye true love, your labour is in vain; Whaur pleisures blossom tak them as ye find For love is leal as weddercock in wind. Adieu, Adieu, Adieu.

(SERGEANTS chase SENSUALITIE away. She and her hand-maids and

[1]unwilling [2]badgers [3]sure

	FUND-JENNET *sit among the poor people.* TEMPORALITIE *addresses the others of his Estait)*
TEMPORALITIE	My lords, ye know the Thrie Estaites, For Common-Weal should mak debates. Let now amang us be devisit Sic acts as by gude men be praisit;
	And for to save us frae murmell[1] Soon, Diligence, fetch us Gude Counsel! For why, he is a man that knaws Baith the Canon and the Civil Laws.
	(DILIGENCE *passes to* GUDE COUNSEL)
DILIGENCE	Father, ye maun incontinent Pass to the Lords of Parliament; For why? They are determinit all, To do naething without counsel.
	(GUDE COUNSEL *goes to* TEMPORALITIE)
GUDE COUNSEL	My lords, God glad the company! What is the cause ye send for me?
MERCHANT	Sit doun and give us your counsel, How we sall slaik the great murmell Of puir people, that is well knawn And as the Common-Weal has shawn.
TEMPORALITIE	And as we knaw it is the King's will That gude remeid be put there-till, Sir Common-Weal, keep ye the bar, Let nane except yoursel come near!
	(JOHN *lays his hand on* POOR MAN)
JOHN	Ye maun let this puir creature Support me for to keep the door. I knaw his name full siccarly, He will complain as weel as I.
GUDE COUNSEL	My worthy lords, sen ye have taen on hand Some reformation to mak into this land, And as ye knaw it is the Kingës mind Wha till the Common-Weal has aye been kind, Though rieve and theft were stanchit weel eneuch, Yet something mair belangës to the pleuch. The Common-Weal maun other ways be stylit,

[1]unrest

GUDE COUNSEL (Contd)	Or by my faith, the King will be beguilit! The puir commons daily as ye may see Declines doun till extreme poverty And are destroyit, without God on them rue!
POOR MAN	Sir, by God's breid, that tale is very true! It is weel kenned I had baith nowt[1] and horse, Now all my gear ye see upon my corse.
CORRECTION	Or[2] I depart, I think to mak ane order!
JOHN	I pray you, sir, begin first at the Border, For how can we fend us against England, When we can nocht, within our native land, Destroy our own Scots common traitor thiefs, Wha to leal labourers daily does mischiefs? Were I a King, my lord, by Goddës wounds, Whae'er held common thieves within their bounds, Wharethrow that, daily, leal men micht be wrangit, Without remeid these chieftains should be hangit!
TEMPORALITIE	What other enemies hast thou? Let us ken.
JOHN	Sir, I complain upon the idle men. For why, sir, it is God's own bidding All Christian men to work for their living. This bene against the strang beggars, Fiddlers, pipers and pardoners, Thae jugglers, jesters and idle couchers,[3] Thae carriers and their quintessencers[4] Thae babble-bearers and thae bards, Thae sweir swingeours[5] with Lords and Lairds. This bene against thae great fat friars, Augustines, Carmelites and Cordeleirs, And all others that in cowls bene clad, Whilk labours nocht and bene weel fed. I mean, not laborand spiritually, Nor for their living corporally. Lyand in dens like idle dogs. I them compare to weel fed hogs. I think they do themselves abuse, Seeing that they the warld refuse; Having professed sic poverty, Syne flees fast frae necessity!
CORRECTION	Whom upon mair will ye complain?
JOHN	Marry, on mair and mair again! For the puir people with cares cries At the misuse of Law's assize: Ane petty pykand thief is hangit

[1]cattle [2]Before [3]gamblers [4]alchemists [5]idle rogues

But he that all the warld has wrangit —
Ane cruel tyrant, ane strang transgressor,
Ane common public plain oppressor —
By bribes, may he obtain favours
Of treasures and compositors,
And throw laws consistorial
Prolix, corrupt and perpetual,
The common people are put sae under,
Though they be puir it is nae wonder!

CORRECTION   Gude John, I grant all that is true,
Your misfortune full sair I rue.
So, my lord Temporalitie,
I you command in time that ye
Expell oppression aff your lands.
Also I say to you Merchands,
If ever I find, by land or sea,
Deceit into your company,
Whilk is to Common-Weal contrair,
I vow to God I sall not spare,
To draw my sword in execution,
And mak on you extreme punition.
My lords, what say ye to this play?

TEMPORALITIE   My sovereign lord, we will obey,
And tak your part with heart and hand,
Whatever ye please us to command.

(Here the TEMPORAL ESTAITES
kneel and say)

MERCHANT   But we beseek you, sovereign,
Of all our crimes that are by-gane,
To give us ane remission!

TEMPORALITIE   And here we mak to you condition
The Common-Weal for to defend,
From henceforth till our livës end.

CORRECTION   On that condition I am content
To pardon you sen ye repent,
The Common-Weal tak by the hand,
And mak with him perpetual band!

(The LORDS *and* MERCHANTS
of the TEMPORAL ESTAITES *embrace*
JOHN THE COMMON-WEAL*)*

John, have ye ony mair debates
Against my lords, the Spiritual Estaites?

JOHN	Na, sir, I dare not speak the sooth,
	Wha plains on priests gets little ruth.
CORRECTION	Flyte on thee fow, fill, I desire thee,
	Sae that thou shaw but the verity!
JOHN	Gramercy, than I sall not spare,
	First to complain on our Vicar.
	The puir cottar being like to die,
	Havand small infants twa or three,
	And has twa kye withouten mair,
	The vicar must have ane of thae,
	With the grey coat that haps the bed,
	Howbeit the wife be puirly cled!
	And gif the wife die on the morn,
	Though all the bairns should be forlorn,
	The other cow he cleeks away,
	With the puir coat of raploch grey.
TEMPORALITIE	Are all thae tales true that thou tells?
POOR MAN	True, sir, the devil stick me else!
	For by the Haly Trinity,
	That same was practisit on me!
JOHN	Our Parson here, he taks nae other pine
	But to receive his tiends and spend them syne!
POOR MAN	Our bishops with their surplices of white,
	They flow in riches royally and delyte;
	Like Paradise bene their palaces and places,
	And wants nae pleasure of the fairest faces!
	But doubt I wad think it ane pleasant life
	Aye when I list to part me from my wife
	Syne tak another of far greater beauty.
	But ever alas, my lords, that may not be,
	For I am bound, alas, in marriage,
	But they like rams rins rudely in their rage!
PARSON	Thou lies, false hure-son raggit loun!
	There is nae priests in all this toun,
	That ever usit sic vicious crafts!
SPIRITUALITIE	(to TEMPORALITIE)
	My lords, why do ye thole[1] that lurdan loun
	Of Kirk-men to speak sic detraction?
	Yon villain puts me out of charity!
TEMPORALITIE	Why, my lord, says he ocht but verity?
	Ye cannot stop ane puir man for till plain!
SPIRITUALITIE	I will not suffer sic words of yon villain!

[1]suffer

POOR MAN	Then gar give me my three fat kye again!
SPIRITUALITIE	False carle, to speak to me stands thou not awe?
POOR MAN	The fiend receive them that first devisit that law! Within an hour after my dad was deid The vicar had my cow hard by the heid!
PARSON	False hure-son carle, I say that law is gude, Because it has been lang our consuetude![1]
POOR MAN	When I am Pape, that law I sall put doun! It is ane sair law for the puir commoun!
SPIRITUALITIE	I mak a vow, thae words thou sall repent!
GUDE COUNSEL	I you require, my lords, be patient! We cam not here for disputation: We cam to mak gude reformation!
JOHN	Did God command that when a puir man dies The Kirk should rob his widow for their fees?
SPIRITUALITIE	We will want naething that we have in use Kirtle nor cow, teind lamb, teind grice nor goose!
TEMPORALITIE	We will decree here that the Kingës grace Sall write unto the Pope's haliness. With his consent, by proclamation, Baith corpse-present[2] and cow we sall cry doun!
SPIRITUALITIE	To that, my lords, we plainly disassent! Note that thereof I tak an instrument!
	(The SCRIBE *notes)*
TEMPORALITIE	My lord, by Him that all the warld has wrocht, We carena whether ye consent or nocht!
MERCHANT	Ye are but ane estait and we are twa, And whaur the greater will, my lord, there aa!
POOR MAN	Och, my lords, for the haly Trinity, Remember to reform the consistory!
PARSON	What cause has thou, false pellour, for to plain ye?
POOR MAN	Therein I happenit amang a greedy menyie! I lent my gossip my mare to fetch hame coals And he her drounit into the quarry holes! They gave me first ane thing they call citandum, Within aucht days I gat but libellandum, Within ane month I gat ad opponendum, In half ane year I gat interloquendum, And syne I gat — how call ye it? — ad replicandum; But I could never a word yet understand him! But or they came half gait to concludendum

---

[1]custom [2]death-due

POOR MAN (Contd)	The fient a plack was left for to defend him. Of pronounciandum they made me wonder fain, But I gat never my gude grey mare again!
TEMPORALITIE	My lords, we maun reform the consistory laws, Whase great defame above the heavens blaws!
MERCHANT	Sae that the King's honour we may advance, We will conclude, as they have done in France. Let spiritual matters pass to Spiritualitie And temporal matters to Temporalitie!
JOHN	My lords, ye have richt prudently concludit! Tak tent now how the land is clean denudit Of gowd and silver whilk daily gaes to Rome, For bribes, mair than the rest of Christendom. Never ane penny should go to Rome at all, Nae mair than did to Peter nor to Paul!
MERCHANT	We merchants, weel I wat, within our bounds Has furnished priests ten hundred thousand pounds, For their finance; nane knaws sae weel as we! Therefore , my lords, devise some remedy! Sir Simony has made with them a band The gowd of weicht they lead out of the land.
GUDE COUNSEL	It is short time sen ony benefice Was sped in Rome, except great bishopries. But now for ane unworthy vicarage, Ane priest will rin to Rome in pilgrimage. Ane cavell,[1] whilk was never at the schule Will rin to Rome and keep ane bishop's mule, And syne come hame with mony colourit crack, With ane burden of benefices on his back — Whilk bene against the law, ane man alane For to possess mair benefices nor ane. Sae I conclude, my lords, and sayis for me Ye should annul all this plurality! Advise, my lords, what think ye to conclude?
TEMPORALITIE	Sir, by my faith, I think it very gude That frae henceforth nae priests sall pass to Rome. Because our substance they do still consume. Also I think it best by my advice That ilk priest sall have but ane benefice.
GUDE COUNSEL	Mark weel, my lords, there is nae benefice Given to a man, but for a gude office! Wha taks office and syne they cannot use it, Giver and taker, I say, are baith abusit. Ane bishop's office is to be ane preacher,

[1] low fellow

	And of the Law of God ane public teacher.
SPIRITUALITIE	Friend, where find ye that we should preachers be?
GUDE COUNSEL	Look what Saint Paul writes into Timothy. Tak there the Buik; let see gif ye can spell!
SPIRITUALITIE	I never read that, therefore read it yoursel!
TEMPORALITIE	Then before God, how can ye be excusit, To have ane office and wats not how to use it? Wherefore were given you all the temporal lands, And all thir teinds ye have amang your hands? They were given you for other causes, I ween, Than mumble matins and haud your claes clean!
MERCHANT	Ye say to the Apostles that ye succeed, But ye shaw nocht that into word nor deed!
JOHN	King James the First, Roy of this region, Said David was a sair saint to the croun. I hear men say that he was something blind, That gave away mair than he left behind[1].
ABBOT	My Lord Bishop, I marvel how that ye Suffer this carle for to speak heresy! For by my faith, my lord, will ye tak tent, Deserves he for to be brunt incontinent! Ye cannot say but it is heresy To speak against our law and liberty!
	(CORRECTION *intervenes and* *addresses* JOHN)
CORRECTION	Shaw furth your faith and feign it nocht!
	(JOHN *pauses before reciting* *this little creed in Scots*)
JOHN	I believe in God that all has wrocht, And create every thing of nocht; And in his Son, our Lord Jesu, Incarnate of the Virgin true; Wha under Pilate tholit passion And deit for our salvation; And on the thrid day rase again, As haly Scripture shawës plain. Also, my lord, it is weel kenned, How He did to the heaven ascend, And set Him doun at the richt hand Of God the Father, I understand; And sall come judge on Doomesday. What will ye mair, sir, that I say?
CORRECTION	Shaw furth the rest: this is nae game!

[1]King David founded many abbeys.

JOHN	I trow *Sanctum Ecclesiam*[1] — But nocht in thir bishops nor thir friars!
MERCHANT	(*to* CORRECTION) I think, my lord, if gude it sa appears, That the King's grace sall give nae benefice But till ane preacher that can use that office. The silly sauls that are Christ Jesus' sheep Should nocht be given to gourmand wolves to keep! What be the cause of all the heresies, But the abusion of the prelacies?
TEMPORALITIE	We think your counsel is very gude, As ye have said, we all conclude! (VERITIE *and* CHASTITIE *come forward to "mak their plaint at the bar"*)
VERITIE	My sovereign, I beseek your excellence, Use Justice on Spiritualitie, The whilk to us has done great violence, Because we did rehearse the verity; They put us close into captivity, Sae we remainit, into subjection, Into great langour and calamity Till we were freed by King Correction!
CHASTITIE	My lord, I have great cause for to complain, I could get nae lodging intill this land; The Spiritual State had me sae at disdain. With Dame Sensuall they have made sic ane band, Amang them all nae friendship, sirs, I fand: And when I came the noble nuns amang, My lusty Lady Prioress frae hand, Out of her dorter durlie she me dang!
CORRECTION	What say ye now, my Lady Prioress? How have ye usit your office, can ye guess? What was the cause ye refusit harboury To this young lusty Lady Chastity? (PRIORESS *at first makes a haughty reply*)
PRIORESS	I do my office after use and wont! To your Parliament, I will mak nae account! (FIRST SERGEANT *steps forward and pulls her from among the SPIRITUAL ESTAIT*)
FIRST	Come on, my Lady Prioress,

---

[1]The Holy Church

SERGEANT	We sall leir you to dance,
	And that within a little space
	Ane new pavane of France!
	(*The* SERGEANTS, *in pulling*
	her habit, haul it off, showing a
	kirtle of silk — a dress —
	under her habit)
SECOND	Now, brother, by the Mass,
SERGEANT	By my judgement, I think
	This haly Prioress
	Is turnit ane cow-clink!
PRIORESS	I give my friends my malison,
	That me compellit to be ane nun,
	And wad nocht let me marry!
	It was my friendës greediness
	That gart me be ane Prioress,
	Now heartily them I wary![1]
	Howbeit the Nuns sing nicht and days,
	Their heart wats not what their mouth says,
	The sooth I you declare,
	Makkand you intimation
	To Christës congregation,
	Nuns are not necessair!
	But I sall do the best I can,
	And marry some gude honest man,
	And brew gude ale in tun!
	Marriage, by my opinion,
	It is better religion,
	As to be friar or nun!
	(KING *and* CORRECTION *whisper*
	with the TEMPORAL ESTAIT)
CORRECTION	With the advice of King Humanitie,
	Here I determine with ripe advisement,
	That all thir prelates sall depryvit be!
KING	As ye have said, but doubt done it sall be!
	(*The* COURTIERS *despoil*
	SPIRITUALITIE)
ABBOT	There is a thousand in the Kirk, but doubt,
	Sic fules as we, gif they were weel socht out!
	Now, brother, sen it may nae better be,
	Let us gae sup with Sensualitie!
	(*They go to* SENSUALITIE,
	who rebuffs them)

[1]curse

SENSUALITIE	Pass frae us, fules, by Him that has us wrocht. Ye lodge not here, because I knaw you nocht!
SPIRITUALITIE	I see nocht else, brother, withouten fail, But this false warld is turnit tap owre tail . . .
ABBOT	There was nae monks frae Carrick to Crail That fared better or drank mair halesome ale. My paramours were baith as fat and fair As ony wench into the toun of Ayr. Allace! this reformation I may wary, For I hae twa dochters for to mairry . . .
PARSON	The deil may care for this unhappy chance! I'll tak my leave withoot a backwart glance. I'll earn my wage amang the men of weir, And win my living with my sword and spear.
	(*Exeunt* SPIRITUALITIE, ABBOT, *and* PARSON *in their undergarments.* SENSUALITIE *turns her attention to* JOHN THE COMMON-WEAL. *He stands transfixed*)
JOHN	Madam, your beauty stounds me wi its straik Could sic a lady be a puir man's maik?
SENSUALITIE	Of thae bag-bellied priests I've wearied sair, Wearied nae less o kings wi little virr . . .
CORRECTION	Gude Counsel, why stand ye sae silent?
GUDE COUNSEL	John, beware! You too may fall her prey And love not truth, but lechery, wine, and play. Great King, I counsel that sans dalliance This sinful lady be harled hame to France.
CORRECTION	As ye devise, it sall be done . . . Sergeants, your duty!
	(*As they advance towards SENSUALITIE*)
SENSUALITIE	Lay not your clawed hands on Sensualitie! Come Hameliness and Danger! Fund-Jennet Come! We needna tarry here! (*to the audience*) Of this new government I wish ye all blithe cheer!
	(*Exeunt* SENSUALITIE, HAMELI- NESS, DANGER *and* FUND-JEN- NET *singing*)

<table>
<tr><td></td><td>(CORRECTION now turns to
FLATTERIE, who is in the
stocks, still disguised as a friar)</td></tr>
<tr><td>CORRECTION</td><td>Sergeant, I counsel you fra hand,
Banish yon friar out of this land,
    And that incontinent!
Yon flatterand knave, withouten fable,
I think he is not profitable,
    I knaw his false intent!</td></tr>
<tr><td>SERGEANT</td><td>Come on, sir friar, and be not fleyit[1]
The King our maister maun be obeyit,
    But ye sall have nae harm.</td></tr>
<tr><td></td><td>(He takes FLATTERIE out of
the stocks, and makes to
lead him away)</td></tr>
<tr><td></td><td>If ye wad travel frae toun to toun,
I think this hood and heavy goun
    Will haud your wame owre warm!</td></tr>
<tr><td></td><td>(He pulls FLATTERIE's habit,
which also comes off)</td></tr>
<tr><td>FLATTERIE</td><td>My lords, for God's sake, let not hang me,
Howbeit these widdiefows[2] wad wrang me!
    I can mak nae debate
To win my meat at plough or harrows —
But I sall help to hang my marrows,
    Baith Falsehood and Deceit!</td></tr>
<tr><td>CORRECTION</td><td>Then pass thy way and graith[3] the gallows!
Syne help for to hang up thy fellows,
    Thou gets nae other grace!</td></tr>
<tr><td></td><td>(The SERGEANTS lead
FLATTERIE back towards the
stocks and gallows)</td></tr>
<tr><td>DECEIT</td><td>Now Flatterie, my auld companion,
What does yon King Correction?
    Knaws thou not his intent?
Declare to us of thy nouvelles!</td></tr>
<tr><td>FLATTERIE</td><td>Ye'll all be hangit, I see nocht else,
    And that incontinent!</td></tr>
<tr><td>DECEIT</td><td>Now waylaway, will ye gar hang us?
The Deil brocht yon curst King amang us,
For meikle sturt and strife.</td></tr>
</table>

[1]afraid   [2]rascals   [3]prepare

FLATTERIE	I had been put to deid amang you,
	Wer't nocht I took in hand to hang you,
	And sae I savit my life!
GUDE COUNSEL	(*To* CORRECTION)
	Or ye depart, sir, aff this region
	Give John the Common-Weal ane gay garmoun,
	Because the Common-Weal has been owrelookit,
	That is the cause that Common-Weal is cruikit.
	With singular profit he has been sae suppressit,
	That he is baith cauld, nakit and disgysit.
CORRECTION	As ye have said, Father, I am content,
	Sergeants, give John ane new aboulyament!
	Of satin, damask or of the velvet fine,
	And give him place into our Parliament syne!
	(*They clothe* JOHN *"gorgeously"*
	and set him down among them
	in the Parliament)
CORRECTION	Blist is the realm that has ane prudent King
	Whilk does delight to hear the veritie.
	There may nae people hae prosperitie
	Whaur ignorance has the dominion
	And Common-weal by tyrants trampit down.
	(POOR MAN *comes forward.*)
POOR MAN	I give you my braid benison,
	That has given Common-weal a goun!
	But I beseek you, for all hallows
	Gar hang Deceit and all his fellows,
	And banish Flatterie aff the toun,
	For there was never sic ane loon!
	(*The* SERGEANTS *loose the*
	prisoners out of the stocks and
	lead them to the gallows.)
FIRST SERGEANT	Come here Deceit, my companion!
	Saw ever a man liker ane loon
	To hing upon ane gallows?
DECEIT	This is eneuch to mak me mangit!
	Dule fall me, that I maun be hangit!
	Let me speak with my fellows!
SECOND SERGEANT	Come here Falsehood and grace the gallows!
	Ye maun hing amang your fellows,
	For your cankart condition.
FALSEHOOD	Alas maun I be hangit too?

What meikle devil is this ado?
How cam I to this, cummer?[1]

SECOND
SERGEANT
Monie ane true man have ye wrangit
Therefore but doubt ye sall be hangit,
But mercy or remission.

(FIRST SERGEANT *presents
halter*)

FIRST
SERGEANT
Stand still. Me thinks ye draw aback!

DECEIT
Alas Maister, ye hurt my craig![2]

FIRST
SERGEANT
It will hurt better, I wad ane plack,
Richt now when ye hing upon the knag!

(*He points to the knag, the
arm of the gallows*)

DECEIT
Adieu my maisters, merchant men,
I have you servit, as you ken,
Truly baith air and late!
I leirit they merchants mony a wile,
The country wives for to beguile
        upon ane mercat day;
And gar them trow their stuff was gude
When it was rotten by the Rood,
And swear it was nocht sae;
To sell richt dear and buy dirt chaip,
        That fashion wasnae folly,
To mix rye-meal amang the saip[3]
And saffron with oyldoilie.[4]
I say to you in conclusion,
I dreid ye gang to confusion
        frae time ye want Deceit.

FALSEHOOD
My gude maisters, ye craftsmen,
Want ye Falsehood, full weil I ken,
        Ye will all die, for hunger!
I leirit tailors in every toun,
To shape five quarters in any goun
        To them I leirit that leir.
Adieu my maisters, wrichts and masons
I need not leir you on ony lessons
        Ye knaw my craft perqueir.[5]
Adieu, I may nae langer tarry
I maun pass to the King of Fairy
        Or else straichtway to Hell.
Farewell, for I am to the widdy[6] wend,
For why, Falsehood made never better end.

[1]friend [2]neck [3]soap [4]olive oil
[5]by heart [6]noose

(FALSEHOOD *and* DECEIT
are hanged)

FLATTERIE

Have I not scapit the widdy weel?
Yea, that I have, by sweet Saint Geill,
      For I had nocht been wrangit,
Because deserved I, by All Hallows,
To have been marshalled with my fellows
      And heich abune them hangit!
When I had on my Friar's Hood,
All men believit I was gude,
But I made far mair faults nor my mates
I beguiled all the Thrie Estaites,
      With my hypocrisie,
Mark weel. My feres hae payed their aa,
But Flatterie slips clean awa,
O aa the warld I'm free!

(*Exit* FLATTERIE *skipping
and laughing.*)

DILIGENCE

Famous people, heartily I you require
This little sport to tak in patience.
We traist in God, an we live another year,
Where we have failit, we sall do diligence,
With mair pleasure to mak you recompence,
Because we have been some part tedious,
With matter rude, denude of eloquence,
Likewise, perchance, to some men odious.
Now, let ilk man his way advance!
Let some gae drink, and some gae dance!
Minstrels, blaw up ane brawl of France!
      Let's see wha hobbles best!
For I will rin, incontinent,
To the tavern or ever I stent.
I pray to God omnipotent,
To send you all gude rest!

(*Minstrels strike up the
"brawl"— a merry dance tune*)

THE END OF ANE SATYRE OF THE THRIE ESTAITES.

ANE SATYRE OF THE THRIE ESTAITES

HISTORICAL NOTE TO THE BIOGRAPHY OF ROBERT KEMP
(Page eight)

The Edinburgh Gateway Company was disbanded in early 1965. The Edinburgh Civic Theatre, which started operations in September 1965, had no direct connection with the old Gateway Company although Robert Kemp had joined the board of the Edinburgh Civic Theatre Trust shortly after its inception the previous year.

ERRATA

Page five, line 31	for playright read playwright
Page thirty-three, line 19 (DECEIT to GUDE COUNSEL)	for hure-soon read hure-son
Page thirty-six, line 14 (CHASTITIE'S SONG)	for *discurssuns* read *discursumus*
Page fifty-nine, line 17 (PARDONER'S SPEECH)	line should read My pardons and my privilege
Page seventy, line 3 (CORRECTION to JOHN)	line should read Flyte on thy fow, fule, I desire thee,